OXFORDSHIRE

COUNTRY WALKS

3

OTMOOR

Mary Webb, Alan Spicer and Allister Smith

Illustrated by Louise Spicer

OXFORDSHIRE
COUNTY COUNCIL
LEISURE & ARTS

First published in 1992 by Oxfordshire Books
Copyright © 1992 Oxfordshire County Council

British Library Cataloguing-in-publication Data

Oxfordshire County Council
Oxfordshire Country Walks. – Vol. 3: Otmoor
I. Title
796.51094257

ISBN 0-7509-0107-1

Produced for
OXFORDSHIRE BOOKS
Official Publisher to Oxfordshire County Council
by
Alan Sutton Publishing Ltd
Phoenix Mill · Far Thrupp
Stroud · Gloucestershire

Cover photograph: Noke Church (*Paul Felix*)

Typeset in Times
Typesetting and origination by
Alan Sutton Publishing Limited
Printed in Great Britain by
The Bath Press, Avon

Contents

23. 5. 93

8. 5. 93

Preface

This series of circular walks explores the Otmoor region extending north-west into the lower Cherwell valley and east to Bernwood Forest and the River Thame, so providing a link with both the Cotswolds and the Chilterns, areas covered by the first two books in the series. Many of the walks include sections of the Oxfordshire Way long distance footpath which crosses the county.

The length of the walks varies from three to six miles (five to ten km) and short cuts are included where possible. The majority of the walks are on level ground but in wet weather some will be muddy. Obviously the time taken to follow the routes will vary with the individual but they are designed to be taken at a leisurely pace allowing plenty of time to read the descriptions and look at the wildlife and landscape. Ordnance Survey maps 1:25000 scale will add to the interest of the trails and grid reference numbers head each section of the route descriptions.

The guide has been produced with the aim of showing how much of our heritage is present in the landscape. You will find features ranging from Roman roads, Domesday Book manors, medieval field remnants, Royal Forest, seventeenth- and eighteenth-century designed landscapes and industrial archaeology to modern developments. The introduction gives a brief background to the history of the landscape and the wildlife of the area.

We hope you enjoy discovering your landscape as much as we enjoyed producing this book.

Introduction

THE PAST IN THE LANDSCAPE

Although many of the variations in the landscape are
gradually being obliterated by modern agriculture
and development, the area covered in this series of
walks divides roughly into two historical types,
formed partly as a result of the differences produced
by their underlying geology.

The majority of the countryside is the ordered
landscape of the seventeenth and eighteenth centuries with regular fields enclosed from the earlier
medieval open fields, interspersed with the great
houses and ornamental parks of the wealthy. Traces
can also be seen of the remnants of Royal Forests
which nearly a thousand years ago were an important influence on this area.

The second type of landscape has its roots in a
humbler past. Otmoor was a large area of land too
wet for agriculture, used by the poor of the surrounding parishes for common land and rough-
grazing and even now requires large scale drainage
to produce profitable crops.

THE ORGANISED LANDSCAPE

Agriculture

On the drier limestone ridges near Islip and Beckley
there is evidence of Roman occupation and agriculture which probably carried on from an earlier

British presence in the area. Many other villages in this area have Saxon origins, those on drier land like Kirtlington, Bletchingdon, Hampton Poyle and Albury probably originating earlier than those in thickly wooded or marshy places like Noke, Fencott and Murcott.

By the time of the Norman invasion and the making of the Domesday Book twenty years later in 1086, all these settlements were in existence and much of the land was in cultivation varying in extent from Bletchingdon, which was using all its available land, to Noke, much of which was still wooded.

During the following medieval period the land was farmed using a system based on large open fields, the number of which varied from place to place and over time. The fields were divided into furlongs which were further subdivided into strips held by individual tenants who were allocated land throughout the fields, so having a share in the good or poor land. Crops were grown in a two or three year rotation with one field remaining unsown or fallow each year to rest it and help to maintain fertility. The land was ploughed so as to produce high ridges which aided water drainage, especially important on the clay soils of much of this area. The remnants of this ridge-and-furrow, which can be seen today, stem from the laying down of arable land for grazing pasture from the fourteenth century onwards. This was partly as a result of the drop in population after the Black Death which reduced the workforce, and also to take advantage of the riches which could be made in wool production.

As time went on more land was cleared from woodland; the fields formed by this are called assarts. In most places this took place in the Middle Ages but in Noke and Islip was not completed until the end of the eighteenth and early nineteenth centuries.

In addition to the arable land most settlements had meadows for hay production, usually situated near a water-course on the rich alluvial soil, as well as some pasture for animal grazing.

Grazing also took place on the arable fields after harvest, on the fallow field and field headlands and edges. Rough grazing was available on the common land, marginal land often too poor for cultivation and where villagers had rights to graze specific numbers of animals.

Parks and Royal Forest

Not all the land was used for farming. At Beckley, Bletchingdon and Kirtlington parks were made from the twelfth to the fourteenth century for the use of the Lord of the Manor to hunt deer. The land within the park was a mixture of trees and grassland known as wood pasture. In the case of Beckley the circular shape of the old park can still be traced on the Ordnance Survey map. A circular shape provided, the maximum internal area with the minimum perimeter fence. The parks at Bletchingdon and Kirtlington were later absorbed into larger landscape schemes.

Another major influence on the landscape of this region were the areas of Royal Forest. To the south lay Shotover Forest and to the east Bernwood Forest. Royal Forest was a legal concept covering an area subject to certain forest laws and kept as a hunting reserve for the king. The land was not all wooded and did not necessarily all belong to the king. The forests produced deer used for stocking parks elsewhere, venison for the king, for gifts and also timber for large construction. Timber from Bernwood Forest was sent as far away as St Albans, Kenilworth and Marlborough. Neighbouring villages had grazing rights in the forests; Murcott had rights in Bernwood Forest whilst Islip, Noke, Beckley and other villages had rights in Shotover, allowing pigs into the forest during the pannage season to eat acorns.

Shotover Forest was established in Saxon times and Bernwood Forest possibly had its origins in the Iron Age but both were disafforested or removed from Forest Law in the seventeenth century when people with rights of common in the Forests were allocated land in compensation.

Enclosure

From the sixteenth century onwards landowners started to enclose their land, not always with the consent of their tenants. Over the next three hundred years all the open fields were enclosed as the more efficient farming methods and improved crops were seen to be of benefit to the landowners. A more flexible type of farming could be used in the smaller hedged fields and gradually the landscape changed from wide open vistas to a new planned countryside with regular shaped fields with straight hedges, new outlying farms and realigned roads. The early enclosures were either imposed on the villagers, as at Bletchingdon in the early seventeenth century, or organised with general agreement by all concerned. Later, Private Acts of Parliament were passed for each particular parish. In the mid-nineteenth century a General Enclosure Act was passed which provided more safeguards for the poor who on the whole were badly affected by enclosure. For example when 130 acres of common land were enclosed at Noke in 1829 there was no compensation for the cottagers in exchange for their loss of common rights. The small amounts of land which they farmed and their common rights of grazing and fuel gathering tended to be lost in the redistribution of the land; from being smallholders the poor became badly paid labourers.

Designed landscapes

Another facet of the general spirit of improvement which swept through the landowning classes in the eighteenth century was manifested in the fashion for landscaping the grounds surrounding their country houses. Many large houses were rebuilt or given a face-lift during this century and what had in many cases been medieval deer-park was transformed into landscaped parkland. The earliest type of landscaping like that which took place at Rycote in the middle of the sixteenth century was quite formal but in the eighteenth century these orderly designs were superseded by a more natural look. Lakes followed the contours of the land and mature trees were placed so as to provide perspective and enhance the view. There were no formal gardens and grass came right up to the houses. Boundaries were hidden with ha-has, sunken walls or fences, and often a focal point was given with the building of a folly in the form of a tower, ruin or obelisk. 'Capability' Brown was the best known designer of this type of landscape and he was responsible for the parks at Rycote, made for the Earl of Abingdon in 1769, and at Kirtlington for Sir James Dashwood between 1751 and 1762, remnants of which can still be seen (Walk 1).

THE LANDSCAPE OF THE POOR

Prior to the enclosure of the open fields and commons, the poor people of a village could make a meagre living by keeping a few animals and grazing them on the common land and by growing crops on the strips of arable allotted to them.

Otmoor

The name of Otmoor means the 'fen of Otta' and this explains why for centuries this large area was used for common land, its wet marshy nature making it unsuitable for agriculture.

Villagers in the seven 'towns' surrounding Otmoor (Beckley, Noke, Oddington, Charlton, Fencott, Murcott and Horton) had the right to graze their animals and collect fuel there in addition to using the common land within their own parishes. Otmoor did not belong to any one parish and none of them claimed to have a greater right to it than any of the others. However, the lords of the manor of Beckley are recorded as having jurisdiction over the use of the Moor, administering the regulations which governed its use. By the sixteenth century these rules had become quite detailed; the right of common on the moor was always linked to the occupancy of particular houses; the numbers of sheep and geese which could graze were strictly controlled or stinted; pigs and hogs had to be ringed to stop them grubbing up the ground; people who had more than a certain income per year were forbidden to collect cow pats for fuel and if caught were fined. All the animals were branded with the first letter of the appropriate township name, the branding iron being kept at Beckley. This was also the meeting place of the Moor Court which was composed of two representatives from each town (Fencott and Murcott sent two between them).

However, when the general move towards enclosure of open fields and commons was underway Otmoor was not forgotten. The first suggestion that the moor should be drained and enclosed came in 1728 from the surveyor of the Abingdon estates. No action was taken but another proposal came from Sir Alexander Croke of Studley Priory in 1787 who was opposed by the Earl of Abingdon, lord of the manor of Beckley, with the support of 340 families from the Otmoor towns. Together they succeeded in defeating plans to put forward a parliamentary bill. Another attempt also failed in 1801 but in 1815 a bill was passed in Parliament which contained plans for the inclosure and drainage of the Moor, the final award being made in 1830.

Each town was allotted a proportion of the land as were the major landowners and churchmen in compensation for loss of rights belonging to the lord of the manor and church tithes. In effect this meant that the poor received little or nothing, losing the income made from keeping geese, wild fowling and fishing. The reduction of the 'moor evil', a disease which affected cattle grazing in the area, was of benefit to the larger farmers rather than the smallholders. The soil, which experts like Arthur Young had predicted would become valuable, was not as fertile as expected, probably gaining what fertility it had from the floodwater which was now much reduced. The implementation of the drainage and hedging of Otmoor proved to be so expensive that only the large landowners could take up the land they had been allotted so all in all the enclosure of Otmoor was not a success.

In 1830 valuable meadow land around Charlton and Oddington was flooded as a result of the diversion of the River Ray to a new course further north (its present route). This event caused general discontent and led to direct action against the enclosure. Dykes were cut by the affected farmers to return the river to its original course, followed by wholesale uprooting of hedges and fences and smashing of gates and bridges. Eventually the militia and the police were called in and many men were arrested and taken to Oxford where they were rescued by the crowds at St Giles Fair. The unrest continued for at least four years.

Until 1920 Otmoor remained as grazing land in private ownership; the rich crops never materialised. After this date part of the moor was acquired by the Royal Air Force for use as a practice bombing range. During the Second World War it was used as a dummy airfield to decoy German bombers. In 1953 a shooting range was built and this together with the danger zone around it have never really been cultivated. In the early 1960's land near Noke was drained with a new series of ditches and pumping equipment and today this is the main agricultural area of Otmoor.

TRANSPORT

Roads

Many of the roads in the area have always been used as such but some have increased in importance over the centuries, whilst others have declined and are now no more than paths or grassy tracks. The oldest paved road in this area is the Roman road across Otmoor but there are several roads which became turnpikes in the eighteenth century and were improved with stones or gravel.

Turnpike Trusts were set up to replace the earlier system whereby each parish was responsible for the upkeep of the roads within its boundaries often leading to the neglect of the main roads little used by local people. The Trusts were an early form of private enterprise set up by people who would gain from improved road conditions. They were allowed to erect gates along the stretch of road for which they had taken responsibility and then to charge tolls which paid for road maintenance and expenses. The road through Islip was an early turnpike set up in 1718.

Some roads date from the enclosures of the eighteenth and nineteenth centuries and can be recognised by their fairly straight route and the characteristically wide grass verges, left to allow for the passage of animals and the generally poor road conditions.

Footpaths which now cross hedged fields probably led between furlongs in the open fields and allowed workers to reach their land; others link settlements but have lost their earlier significance as, for example, the path from the west end of Noke to Islip, probably a medieval 'corpse way' (see p. 49).

Oxford Canal

The Oxford Canal which winds through the Cherwell valley was one of the earliest and most important in southern England. It was first approved in 1769 to carry coal from Warwickshire to Banbury and Oxford and to link the River Thames with the Grand Union Canal south of Coventry. James Brindley was appointed engineer but died in 1772 before the canal was completed. The canal reached Banbury in 1778 but took another twelve years to be completed to Oxford, opening in 1790. This section was designed by Robert Whitworth who made use of part of the river just north of Shipton-on-Cherwell.

The northern section was modernised in the 1820's but the first fifty miles from Oxford remain as designed by Brindley and is typical of a canal of the 1770's. The brick bridge at Shipton-on-Cherwell indicates the then 'modern' style of the canal company as widespread brickmaking was relatively new. Further upstream local limestone is used for bridges and canal buildings as at Kirtlington, situated on a band of oolithic limestone. The lifting bridge at Thrupp is also typical of this part of the Oxford canal, used because they were cheaper than conventional bridges. The coming of the canal meant a huge reduction in the price of fuel; coal transported by canal only cost 11d per hundredweight, less than 5p in modern terms. This cheap transport and fuel affected both road transport systems and industry and marks the beginning of the industrial age in this part of Oxfordshire.

Railways

Railways came to this part of the county after the rapid expansion of the railway network in the 1840's. The line north from Oxford to Birmingham was opened in 1852 but only after much acrimonious bidding between rival railway companies. The original plan of the Great Western company was to link Oxford with Rugby, but eventually the present route was approved. The other controversy concerned the gauge of the track. Great Western used 7 ft broad gauge but there was pressure from other companies to stop extension of this into the Midlands where 4 ft 8 in standard gauge was widespread. Compromise was reached when Great Western proposed a mixed gauge with three rails to cater for all types of rolling stock and it was this track which was finally laid. All GWR broad gauge was changed to standard gauge track by 1892.

The now disused line between Thame and Oxford was built as part of a new, more direct line between London and the West Midlands joining the main Paddington-Birmingham line south of Oxford. Laid as broad gauge when it opened in 1864, it was one of the first to be converted to standard gauge in 1870.

The coming of the railways had a much wider impact on the general population than did the canals. Not only was transport of goods and industrial products made far more efficient and speedy but travel was now available for everyone with commuting to work and seaside holidays a possibility for all. Now in the late 20th century railways have given way to private cars and the motorway network, with a far greater impact on the environment.

GEOLOGY

The landscape we see today has been greatly influenced in its development by the underlying geological strata. In central Oxfordshire all the solid rock layers were laid down in the Jurassic period, about 180 to 150 million years ago, when the area had a climate similar to the present day Bahamas.

The earliest rocks present are limestones which formed on the floor of the shallow sea covering the area. Known as Great Oolite, these limestones are found around Kirtlington and Islip. Immediately on top of this rock is a layer of harder, rubbly limestone, rich in fossils, known as Cornbrash which forms the ridge bordering the north-west of Otmoor at Charlton-on-Otmoor and Oddington.

Sea levels rose, effectively lowering the sea floor by about 100 m. This removed the effects of tides and currents and allowed dark coloured clay and silts to be deposited, inhabited by oysters and ammonites which could tolerate the oxygen-poor conditions. These conditions lasted for about 8-10 million years and, as the sea floor continued to subside, allowed about 100 m of, what we now call, Oxford Clay to accumulate.

In time conditions changed again and the muddy seas gave way to clear, shallow, well-oxygenated water. A variety of sediments were deposited including sands, limestones made of broken shell debris and the remains of small coral reefs. These sediments are called the Corallian and form much of the higher ground around Oxford and the southern edge of Otmoor.

Further profound geological and climatic changes have taken place since then. As a result of continental plate movements, the seas have withdrawn and the strata tilted and eroded. In geologically more 'recent' times there have been three periods of glaciation during the last two million years. The first two were the most extensive but it is thought that the ice-sheets did not cover this area. However deposits of pebbles and gravel resulted from the rivers carrying meltwater and debris; Bletchingdon and Kirtlington are built on gravel plateaux laid down on the underlying eroded limestone.

The river valleys of the Oxford plain developed after these earlier periods of glaciation. In the area covered by this book, two, namely the Ray and the Thame, flow along the Oxford Clay outcrops while the third, the Cherwell, has carved its way through the limestone before reaching the clay vale north of Kidlington.

During the warmer periods between glaciations, because of higher flow rates, the rivers eroded and deepened their valleys while during colder periods they became infilled with gravel. Subsequent erosion resulted in the formation of the present river terraces. Since the end of the last ice age about 10,000 years ago, alluvium composed of fine silt, has been deposited on the present valley floors. The flat area of Otmoor itself has been formed by flood action of the Ray as a result of its being impeded at Oddington and Islip where it passes through narrow 'gorges'.

For many centuries the various rock formations in the area have been exploited. The Great Oolite limestone around Kirtlington and Shipton-on-Cherwell has been quarried for cement manufacture while the harder Corallian limestone was, for several hundred years, an important source of building stone. The high organic content of Oxford Clay makes it almost self-firing, so it was extensively used for brick making; there were several brick works close to Oxford including one at Horton-cum-Studley which closed in 1930.

NATURAL HISTORY

The most interesting sites for wildlife in the area covered by this book are all remnants of a time when agriculture had a low impact on natural vegetation and associated animal and insect life. Now agricultural methods are more intensive so the natural areas have reduced in size but there is still plenty to be seen.

Wetlands

Although Otmoor as a wildlife site has been adversely affected by modern drainage techniques, much of it is still rough marshy pasture despite nineteenth century attempts to 'improve' the area.

The central area is a Site of Special Scientific Interest (SSSI) ironically protected by the activities of the Ministry of Defence. It is the wettest part of the moor and is regularly under water during the winter and spring. Such conditions restrict agricultural activity and the limited disturbance by machinery and animals over many years has allowed the survival of many uncommon or rare plants and insects specially adapted for life in a waterlogged environment.

Curlew

This wet habitat is a quiet haven for many birds especially in winter when large flocks of ducks, geese and waders rest, feed and shelter in the flooded fields and the larger drainage ditches. The area is well known and appreciated by bird-watchers, with rarities often recorded.

Dragonfly

The flooded meadows provide very different conditions for wildlife compared with the drainage ditches of various sizes and depths, the faster flowing streams and rivers and the slow-moving, steep banked canal. These differences are reflected in the range of plants, insects, birds and animals encountered and described along these walks.

Rivers

The three rivers in the area covered by these walks – the Ray, the Cherwell and the Thame – are for the most part surrounded by agricultural land and have themselves been 'improved' to reduce flooding. Nevertheless they are important sites for wildlife both in the water and on the river banks. The gradual change from dry land to water results in a variety of habitats which provide opportunities for plants and animals with differing requirements. The rivers, with their associated drainage channels, also act as wildlife corridors and often link one area of wildlife value with another, an important factor in the mostly agricultural landscape.

Grassland

The drier parts of Otmoor and other areas nearby were used for hay meadows and this practice of regular cutting followed by grazing for part of the year established a specialised group of plants which flower in early summer and set seed before mowing in July. An example of this can be seen at Bernwood Meadow (Walk 8) and Asham Mead (Walk 7). In order to maintain this rich display of flowers the traditional management needs to be continued or coarser grasses and scrub will gradually take over the grassland. Highly managed grazing fields also have their wildlife value as good foraging areas for flocks of rooks and jackdaws searching for insects and other food.

Hedges and green tracks

Hedges in this area vary in age. Some are relics of woodland clearance or were planted during Tudor enclosures while many others are relatively recent, dating from the time of nineteenth century Parliamentary enclosures. No matter how old, they are all valuable for wildlife, as food sources, shelter, undisturbed habitats for breeding and perhaps most importantly as links between one natural site and another, so allowing plants and animals to spread or colonise new sites. The grassy tracks on Otmoor and other areas perform a similar function in providing shelter especially for butterflies and birds, while their usually natural verges act as small nature reserves for plants and associated insects.

Woodland

The natural vegetation which would cover this part of Britain without any human interference is woodland, the dominant tree species depending on local ground conditions. With the advent of man this 'wildwood' as it is known, was gradually cleared to make way for settled agriculture; it is estimated that the area of woodland cover today is roughly what it was during the Roman occupation.

Some of today's woodland can be classified as ancient, having had a history of continuous tree cover since at least AD 1600 and in most cases much longer. Before this century woods were managed to provide a variety of products ranging from large timber trees for construction work to a steady supply of small poles and wood produced by coppicing for farm and household uses.

During the twentieth century these traditional methods have fallen into disuse and large tracts of deciduous woodland, including Bernwood Forest and Whitecross Green Wood, were cleared in the 1950s and '60s by the Forestry Commission and replanted with fast-growing conifers. These shaded out the original ground flora, and the associated butterfly and moth populations for which these woods were famed were under threat. Modern forestry now works with conservation, and management of the conifer plantations on these ancient woodland sites aims to reinstate suitable habitats for plants and insects by widening rides, mowing verges in rotation, creating glades and, where possible, gradually replacing the conifers with oaks and other native species (see Walks 7 and 8).

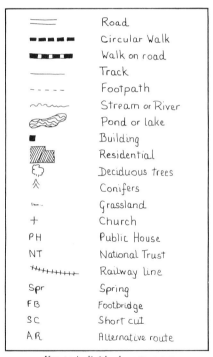

═══	Road
▬ ▬ ▬ ▬	Circular Walk
▬▬▬▬	Walk on road
────	Track
-----	Footpath
∿∿∿	Stream or River
◯	Pond or lake
■	Building
▨	Residential
☘	Deciduous trees
⋏	Conifers
⌐.	Grassland
+	Church
PH	Public House
NT	National Trust
╫╫╫╫	Railway line
Spr	Spring
FB	Footbridge
SC	Short cut
AR	Alternative route

Key to individual route maps

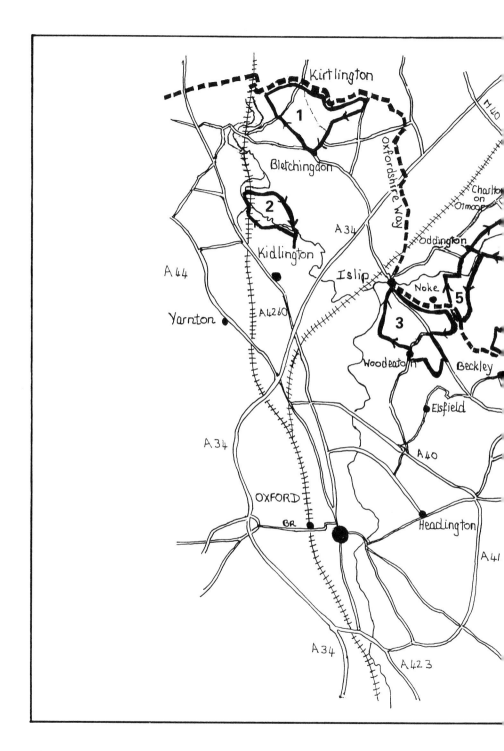

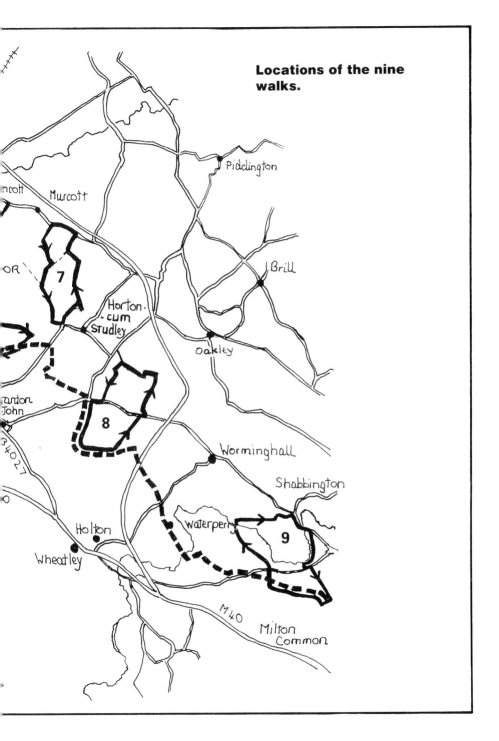

Locations of the nine walks.

Piddington

ncott Murcott

OR 7

Horton·
·cum
Studley

Brill

Oakley

anton
John

4027

8

Worminghall

Shabbington

Holton

Waterperry

9

Wheatley

M40 Milton
Common

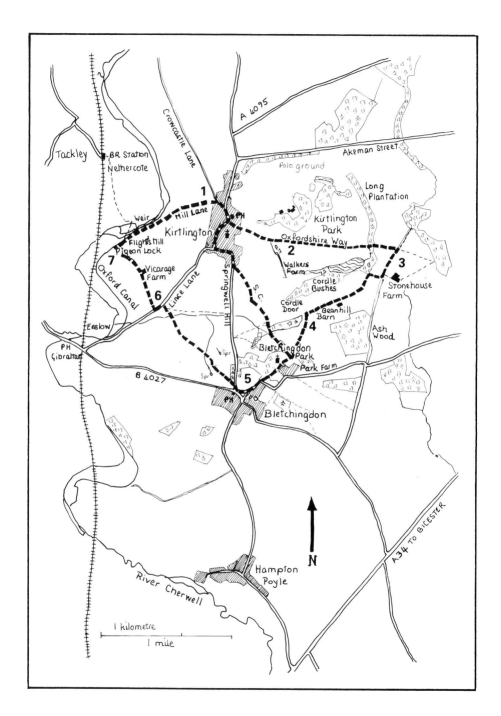

Tackley

BR Station
Nethercote

Crowcastle Lane

A 4095

Akeman Street

Polo ground

Long
Plantation

Kirtlington
Park

Weir   Hill Lane

Flights Mill
Pigeon Lock

Kirtlington

1

PH

Oxfordshire Way

2

7

Oxford Canal

Vicarage
Farm

6

Line Lane

Springwell Hill

Walkers
Farm

S.C.

Cordle
Bushes

Cordle
Door

Beanhill
Barn

3

Stonehouse
Farm

4

Ash
Wood

Enslow

PH
Gibraltar

B 4027

Spr

Spr

Bletchingdon
Park

Park Farm

5

PH PO

Bletchingdon

N

River Cherwell

Hampton
Poyle

A34 TO BICESTER

1 kilometre

1 mile

Kirtlington

6 miles 10 km

Short cut 4.5 miles 7km

This walk uses part of the Oxfordshire Way as it crosses the parkland of Kirtlington House. More eighteenth century parkland is seen at Bletchingdon before crossing old fields to the Oxford Canal on the return to Kirtlington. The going is easy throughout the walk.

1 SP501197

The walk starts from Mill Lane. Walk towards the village and cross the main road, turning right past the school. At the village green opposite the pub turn left and follow the signs for the Oxfordshire Way. You will soon see the village hall ahead on the right, but you must climb the stile in the fence on the left. From the stile follow the Oxfordshire Way, bearing slightly right across the open grassland. Cross a gravel track and continue until the path crosses left into the next field over a bridge and a stile in the fence.

As you walk across the grassland, notice how lush the growth is after having been 'improved' with fertilizer and vigorous growing agricultural grasses. However the thick grass swamps many flowering plants so there is little variety here. One exception is

Kirtlington village green

dandelion. In spring see how the large, strong leaves push aside the grass to enable it to grow successfully. Dandelions are very attractive to insects which readily transfer pollen over the flowers. By a peculiar mechanism called apomixis, the pollen does not fertilise the egg (seed) but has to be present to stimulate seed development. The seeds on all the clocks from one plant are therefore very similar to each other as they are products of only the mother plant. Close clusters of dandelion plants tend to share similar leaf shapes showing that they are related, but are often different to those of other nearby groups.

In late summer long-legged adult crane flies emerge from the soil where their larvae, known as leather jackets, have been feeding for months on grass roots.

Continue in the same general direction across the next field towards a strip of scrubby trees in the opposite corner.

All the land you pass through in this section of the walk was part of the park belonging to Kirtlington House. The earliest park was probably made in 1279 from part of the East Field, one of the two large medieval fields belonging to Kirtlington. This park would have have been used for hunting deer and small game. The park was enlarged and landscaped by Capability Brown between 1755 and 1762 for the Dashwood family and although much is now agricultural land there are still many large trees and an open landscape reminiscent of his original design.

2 SP512191

Cross through the scrubby area into the next field and follow the Oxfordshire Way across the field roughly parallel to the lake, heading towards a stile over a wall.

A clear stream leads into a lake created as part of the landscaped park, visible from Kirtlington House situated on the slope to your left. The lake is bordered by plants which are specific to this water-logged habitat. Water plantain, reed mace, rushes and sedges all have special air-filled spaces inside them so that the roots don't 'drown' and the plants die; oxygen is a necessity even for water-loving plants such as these. The shallow border of the lake

Great crested grebe on nest

beyond the stream is filled with reed-beds which are being invaded by willow. This 'carr' area is part of the natural succession which leads over time to the formation of dry land and over many centuries to the climax vegetation of lowland England which is woodland. The word 'carr' comes originally from an Old Norse word 'kjarr' meaning brushwood. A later derivation came to mean a marsh, especially one overgrown with brushwood.

You may see great crested grebes nesting on the lake. These birds have a fascinating head-bobbing courtship display, often holding clumps of water-weed in their beaks as the pair face each other. The lake is also an excellent habitat for herons, swans and coots.

Climb the stile, cross a track and continue straight on into woodland.

The woodland strip is called Long Plantation and once formed the boundary of the park. Now planted with conifers the ground flora is sparse but some spring flowers can still be found including bluebells, bugle and arum (Lords-and-Ladies). The flowers of this last plant are very attractive to small insects called moth flies. The central column generates its own heat and gives off a smell like rotting meat, enticing the insects into the sheath-like flower. They fall into the swollen flower base and are trapped by a ring of hairs. The insects move about and in so doing pollinate the flower, after which the hairs wilt to allow the flies to escape. In the autumn bright orange spikes of berries are produced which are eaten by birds but are poisonous to humans.

The path emerges onto a field. Go straight over the field and when a hedged track is reached, turn right.

3   SP521193

Turn right along the track and continue until Stonehouse Farm is reached.

This track was once more important than now. It

is shown on Richard Davis's map of 1797 as part of a road which led from close to Gosford Bridge over the River Cherwell linking with the main road to Northampton, now the A34, but is now no more than a green lane.

Bordered by flower-filled verges and old hedges containing a rich diversity of species, it is a valuable corridor for wildlife in an intensively farmed landscape. Many butterflies collect in this sheltered lane. Sunny spring days encourage small whites, green veined whites with black marks outlining the wing veins on the underside, orange-tips (only the males have the orange wing tips), bright yellow brimstones, tortoiseshells, peacocks and commas. Occasionally, harmless grass snakes may be seen on nearby banks, easily recognised by their yellow neck markings.

Stonehouse Farm is one of several outlying farm houses which were built in Bletchingdon parish in the seventeenth century. Unusually for this part of Oxfordshire, Bletchingdon's open fields were enclosed very early, some prior to 1544, in order to convert arable land to sheep pasture and to increase the demesne lands i.e., the holdings of the lord of the manor. This led to local discontent, culminating in a revolt in 1596 when 300 men threatened to sack the Lord of the Manor's house and 'tear down his hedges and those that made them'. However the enclosure continued and was completed by the early seventeenth century.

At the farm leave the main track and turn right for a short distance.

Look out for white deadnettle and stinging nettle, two plants often found in close proximity. Despite the names, they are not closely related, although the leaves of deadnettle are similar in appearance to those of stinging nettles but without the stinging hairs. It has been suggested that this may be an example of plant mimicry, thus animals do not eat the deadnettle leaves mistaking them for stinging nettle.

Grass snake

Just before woodland is reached you will come to two gates on the left. Go through the second and walk up the track through two fields keeping the hedge on the left. After $\frac{1}{3}$ mile (1 km) the path crosses through the hedge on the left via a well-hidden stile just before a patch of scrub.

Walking through these fields in autumn you will see and hear many pheasants which have been reared as game birds and consequently are fairly tame. The patches of sunflowers or brassicas often seen in field corners are grown to provide the birds with food during the winter.

4 **SP510186**

Over the stile take the path bearing slightly right uphill towards Bletchingdon House. This part of the trail is another area of parkland, this time belonging to Bletchingdon House. A park was first recorded here as early as 1322 and was enlarged in the 16th century. The house was an important centre during the Civil War with the King's forces surrendering to Cromwell here in 1644. Earlier, in the 14th century, this was the chief seat of Roger Damory and his wife Elizabeth de Clare, the foundress of Clare College, Cambridge.

Pass through a gate and continue straight on.

Bletchingdon churchyard

SHORT CUT If you turn right here and follow the footpath it will take you back to Kirtlington.

Continue past a renovated stable block and Bletchingdon Church. The church of St Giles dates from the 15th century but is much restored. The earliest record of a church here was a grant of tithes in 1074 by Robert d'Oilley, the Sheriff of Oxford and a figure who had an important influence on all parts of the county. The churchyard today is full of spring-flowering cowslips, primroses, buttercups and speedwell with mossy paths and lichen encrusted tombstones. Contrast it with the newer cemetery across the road which is less rich in wild life.

Follow the path to the village.

The church was enclosed in the ornamental park and this path linking it to the village was only declared a right of way in 1795 after much argument and struggle by the local population.

Polypody fern

Bletchingdon village scene

Go through the kissing gate and straight on along the road towards the green.

In the wall which borders the lane look for polypody ferns, mosses and lichens as well as various flowering plants. One, ivy-leaved toadflax, has an interesting way of ensuring that its seeds stay in the wall. After the purple flowers are finished, see how the flower stalks curl back towards the shady wall and grow into crevices before shedding the seeds, thus providing them with suitable habitats for the next generation.

Continue in the same general direction along the edge of the green to the main road where the trail turns right.

Cottages line two sides of the green but those on the third (north) side were pulled down when Bletchingdon Park was extended in the sixteenth century, presumably when the church was taken into the park. The small building on the edge of the green was a smithy. The main road used to be part of the route from Worcester to London and in the seventeenth century was known as London Way (see Walk 3).

5   SP502177

At the junction just past The Black's Head, look for a signed footpath leading through a gap in the wall at the apex of the junction between the main road and the Kirtlington road. The path leads through a belt of conifers, over a stile and then diagonally right across the field. Cross into the next field where the path leads diagonally to the right, entering a further field through a gap in the hedge. Go straight over this field. At the far side the path crosses a plank bridge and continues over a pasture field to the road.

All the fields in this area remain as they were about four hundred years ago when they were enclosed from the medieval open field. The first field crossed was Sand Furlong which bordered onto Whitemarsh Furlong, probably named after divisions or furlongs in the open field and possibly reflecting local soil conditions.

6 SP491185

Cross the road with care and walk left for a short distance before taking a farm lane to the right. Follow this lane for about half a mile (0.75 km).

The lane is bordered with many calcium-loving plants including purple flowered knapweeds, delicately leaved bedstraws, yarrow with tiny white flowers in dense flat heads and cinquefoil, from the French for five leaved, a member of the rose family. In late summer and autumn the hedgerow is ablaze with colourful fruits and berries of hawthorn, rose and bramble. There is an old country story that many berries foretell a hard winter; it is less romantic but more likely that, plentiful berries and fruits only reflect the previous favourable spring and summer growing season.

Through the yard, bear left and follow the track downhill with a mixed hedge on the right containing hawthorn, dog rose and sloe. The other name for sloe is blackthorn because of its dark coloured sharp spines, especially noticeable in the early spring in contrast to the white blossom which flowers before the leaves have come out.

In May and June search carefully through the young leaves in the hedge and you will find all sorts of caterpillars of butterflies and moths. Some are carefully camouflaged, others very colourful, two methods of protection against predation. Be wary of very hairy ones as they may cause an irritating rash if handled, another defence against being eaten.

7 SP487194

At the bottom of the hill turn right to return directly to Kirtlington or left for a look at the canal and lock.

The canal links Banbury and Oxford and was built between 1785 and 1790 as were the bridge and lock.

Narrow boat entering Pigeons Lock

Pigeons Lock, named after the Three Pigeons pub which has now disappeared, allows for 8 ft 4 in (2.5 m) rise or fall in water level. The canal had a huge impact on the local communities when it was opened. It carried supplies of cheap coal from the Midlands and substantially reduced the wagon traffic on the Worcester-London road. The coal was of benefit to local people who previously had to rely on scanty supplies of wood. However there were problems; flooding caused by inadequate drainage ruined some of the best meadows in Bletchingdon.

Retrace your steps for a short distance and follow the track uphill to Kirtlington.

A little further along the track is the site of Flight's Mill situated on a mill stream from the river close to the far side of the canal. Originally there were two mills here, on sites recorded in the Domesday Book of 1086, one on each side of the river.

The track is bordered by thick hedges with several

33

plants such as bluebells, dog's mercury and goldi-locks buttercup which indicate that originally this area was woodland, only the hedges were left when it was cleared. The track must date from at least the time that the first mills were built more than 900 years ago.

As the track climbs there are more signs of past industrial activity on the left. Large disused quarries now overgrown with trees and vegetation can be seen where limestone was extracted for the cement industry. Thirty six acres were leased to the Oxford Portland Cement Co Ltd and were later sold to them in 1922. Although these are now disused, the cement industry is still active further down the river valley.

At the top of the track you are back at your starting point.

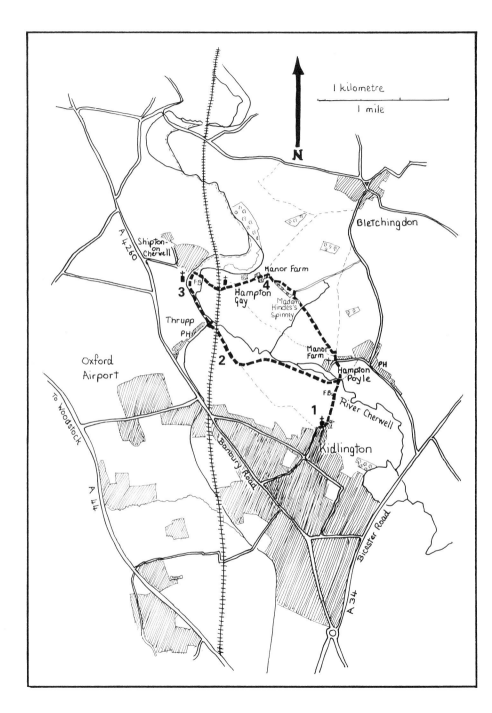

Kidlington

4 miles 6.5 km

This walk leads along a peaceful river bank to meet the Oxford Canal at Thrupp. After following the towpath to Shipton-on-Cherwell the trail continues through quiet fields to the two hamlets of Hampton Gay and Hampton Poyle before returning to Kidlington, said to be the largest village in England. Easy walking over level ground with a series of stiles in the last mile.

1 SP498148

Starting near St Mary's Church walk past the church to the end of the road and climb the stile.

The churchyard is bordered with lime and plane trees. Lime has distinctive soft rounded leaves and in summer bears sweet smelling greenish-yellow flowers much enjoyed by bees. They can get quite drunk on the nectar and can sometimes be found in a lethargic state on the ground beneath the trees. The flowers are borne on long stalks projecting from narrow leaf-shaped parachutes which, when the fruits are ripe, make them spin as they fall from the trees. This slows their fall, giving them a chance to be blown further away from the parent tree for a better chance of survival. Plane leaves resemble maple or sycamore but are covered with hairy down.

Planes can also be distinguished by thin peeling bark said to be one reason why they grow well in cities as pollution on the trunks is shed when the bark falls off. The fruits are much larger than lime and look like round balls dangling on long stalks.

Opposite the churchyard are the Kidlington Almshouses, founded in 1671 – see the datestone over a door – by Sir William Morton in memory of his wife Anne. The names over the windows are of some of their children. The houses have been in occupation since then with few changes until some modernisation took place in the 1950s.

Follow the path straight ahead down the field.

In the first field are many wild flowers which in summer attract numerous meadow browns and other butterflies. Look out for patches of horse radish with large dark green leaves looking similar to dock. Although the leaves have a strong smell it is the roots which are used for making the traditional sauce.

At an opening in the hedge beside a large ditch, bear left over a foot-bridge then right to continue in the same direction as before. This path is an old link with Bletchingdon via Hampton Poyle across the river. A bridge has crossed the Cherwell here since the Middle Ages when it was a wooden structure; the present concrete bridge was built in 1947.

Turn left here and follow the path along the river bank for about one mile (1.5 km).

The flowing water of the Cherwell is home to a specialised community of plants well adapted to waterside and aquatic life like reeds, reed grass, flote grass, water lilies, eel grass and crowfoot. Apart from water lilies with tough rounded leaves, many species tend to have elongated narrow leaves which are not easily damaged by the water current. When submerged, oxygen can be absorbed from the water and held in large spaces inside the stems and leaves, helping the plant to float as well as to breathe. Along the water edge is a different collection of plants which like wet soil but not immersion. Yellow cress

Sedge warbler

with serrated leaves, great willow herb, meadow sweet and hemp agrimony all have broad expansive leaves to capture sunlight for photosynthesis.

The continuous chattering of sedge warblers in the reeds can be heard in late spring and male reed buntings with their smart black heads and ruddy brown backs are often seen. Swans and moorhens also frequent these waters making raised nests amongst the reeds and other vegetation. The neck lengths of different species of waterfowl enable them to reach down to feed at different depths below the water surface so reducing competition for available food. Ahead of you is a well developed meander in the river where it makes a deep loop in the flat valley. It used to be said that these occur as a result of an outcrop of harder rock but now the theory is that they develop in alluvial ground which allows the river to increasingly erode the soil. As the bend develops the stronger current on the outside of the curve erodes the banks and material is deposited on the inside of the curve. Whatever the reason this is a very attractive spot with white flowering water crowfoot growing in the shallow water.

The path bears left across this field to the far corner. Cross into the next field over a small footbridge and head right to the railway bridge close to the river.

2 SP485159

The path goes through a tunnel under the railway which was completed in 1850. Notice on the stonework of the tunnel entrance the spreading yellow lichens which can survive on bare rock because of their low nutrient needs and slow growth rate.

Walk past cottages to the canal at Thrupp.

Thrupp is a hamlet which flourished as a result of the building of the Oxford Canal in the late 1780's linking the Midlands with Oxford. There was a canal basin and wharf here and this wide section of canal allowed traffic to pass while others unloaded. There are still narrow boats to be seen here but now mainly holiday craft with the occasional houseboat.

Turn right and follow the towpath to Shipton-on-Cherwell. (For refreshments take a diversion; go over the lifting bridge and then left for a pub.)

Along this part of the walk notice how the canal designer made use of the natural formation of the landscape as the canal follows the line of the Cherwell valley where the contours are reasonably shallow. At the time these routes were constructed local people felt that they exacerbated the flooding which already occurred in this area but later modifications helped to stop the problem. In winter the difference in height between the canal and the river on the right can clearly be seen.

The waterside vegetation of the canal contrasts

Oxford Canal near Thrupp

with that of the fast-flowing river. There are large beds of reeds on the far side of the canal. These were used in the past for thatching and floor covering, but recently a new use has been found in helping to clean contaminated land because of the ability of this plant to pass air down into the roots. This encourages bacteria around the roots which help to break down polluting chemicals. There are few other plant species along the canal since the slow-moving water lacks oxygen and because the sides and bottoms are regularly dredged to allow passage for boats. Nevertheless this sluggish water favours coarse fish like perch, roach, bream and carp but is not suitable for trout (see Walk 9).

In summer you are likely to see swallows and martins swooping low over the surface catching the insects that hover over the water.

3 SP481165

On the opposite bank, below Shipton-on-Cherwell church, the wider area of towpath was once a wharf for unloading coal for use in the village. (To see the church cross the brick bridge.)

At the bridge turn right down a short track. Climb the stile and bear slightly left across the field to the footbridge over the river.

If you are lucky you may catch a glimpse of a brilliant blue kingfisher, birds which tend to be associated with clean water. This field may be sheep grazed and most plants here grow close to the ground so that they are difficult to eat. Animals eat in different ways which affects where they can be kept. Sheep nibble close to the ground with their front teeth making the most of low or thin vegetation, whereas cattle and horses use their lips more and cannot get so close to the ground so need a lusher growth in rich pasture land.

Cross the bridge and head for the distant white stile which leads over the railway.

On the skyline to the left the tall chimneys belong

to a cement works evidence of the continued use of limestone products in this area (see Walk 1).

Near here the GWR's worst railway disaster took place on Christmas Eve in 1874. Thirty-four people were killed and 69 injured when the 10 o'clock train from Paddington to Birkenhead was derailed and many carriages tumbled down the embankment.

Cross the track. WALK WITH CARE HERE IN CASE OF TRAINS.

Once over the railway you will see the church of Hampton Gay on the left. A church is first recorded here in 1074 but the present church was built in 1767-72 by Revd Thomas Hindes and nothing is left of the earlier building except the battlements and the cross on the east gable. The Hindes family bought the manor in 1691 and their presence in the area is still marked by the name of a small patch of woodland known as Madam Hindes's Spinney which you will skirt in a while.

More information on Hampton Gay can be found on the boards near the church or at the far end of this field.

From the high ground round the church many bumps and hollows are visible in the field, all that is left of a once much larger settlement. As in so many other places in Oxfordshire this manor was enclosed in the sixteenth century for sheep grazing, dis-possessing many local villagers. Feelings ran so high here that in 1596 a revolt was planned which aimed to destroy the enclosures and those responsible for them, before marching to London where the protes-ters hoped for help from the apprentices. In the event only ten people met and, thanks to a spy in the camp, five were arrested and sent to London where one was hanged and quartered. Nevertheless, this small revolt influenced Parliamentary opinion result-ing in the Tillage Act of 1597 which ordered that land in Oxfordshire converted to pasture since the accession of Queen Elizabeth I in 1558 should be restored to crop growing.

As you walk up the field towards the cottages you

Butcher's broom

pass the ruins of the manor house which was built in the second half of the sixteenth century. It remained unaltered until a fire destroyed it in 1887. Beyond the house on the river was a mill which in 1681 was leased to a paper maker, this trade continuing until 1887. Ten years earlier in 1877 a fire had destroyed the roof which was replaced by corrugated iron brought by canal from Bristol at a cost of £610. After the closure of the paper mill the population dropped drastically and now the hamlet is very small.

Close to the ruins, below an imposing group of horse chestnut trees, are clumps of butcher's broom *Couldn't find.* which in the wild are only found in ancient woodland. The dark green 'leaves' are really flattened stems, shown by the position of the flowers and red berries which appear to grow in the centre of the leaf. Rushes also produce flowers along their long narrow 'leaves' which again are modified stems.

4   SP489165

Walk along the road for about half a mile (0.75 km) past two bends. At the third bend, where the field is *through field* open on the right-hand side, cross the field to a stile *of broad beans* at the far corner of the woodland (Madam Hindes's Spinney). Turn left and follow a path through three fields keeping the hedge on your left, over stiles and footbridges until you emerge at the top of a gently sloping field leading down to Manor Farm on the edge of Hampton Poyle.

This field is a classic example of ridge and furrow. Enclosed before 1625 to provide pasture for sheep and cattle, the shape of the ridges are preserved in land which is unlikely to have been ploughed since the late Middle Ages. Further into the distance there is a fine view of the spire of Kidlington church behind the willows lining the River Cherwell. *I lost the path here*

Walk diagonally left down the field looking out for *walked up & down field* a stile on the left almost at the bottom. Over the stile *for ½ h looking for* *way through — ended up with very wet feet after misjudging a log stepping stone.*

44

Sign for FP seems to have been vandalised. FP at left side of field but not marked!

*Kidlington church across the
River Cherwell*

*piched up
track here* →

turn right, climb the next stile, and head down to the
road with the thirteenth century church on the right.
Cross the road and climb into the next field, heading
for the stile leading to the river. Cross the bridge and
retrace your steps to the start in Kidlington.

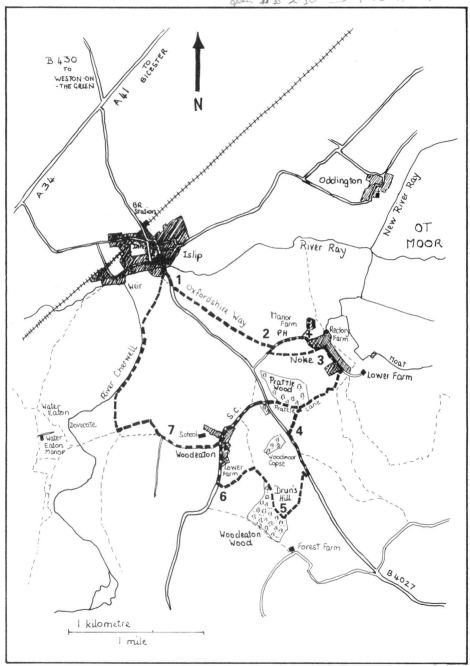

PH at Noke — THE PLOUGH
open 11 to 2.30 — 7.00 - 11.00.

B 430
TO
WESTON-ON
-THE GREEN

A 41
TO
BICESTER

N

A 34

BR
Station

Islip

Weir

Oddington

New River Ray

OT
MOOR

River Ray

1
Oxfordshire Way

Manor
Farm
2 PH

Rectory
Farm

Noke 3

Moat

Lower Farm

River Cherwell

Prattle
Wood

Prattle Lane

Water
Eaton

Dovecote

S.C.

4

Water
Eaton
Manor

7 School

Woodeaton

Woodmoor
Copse

Lower
Farm

Drun's
Hill

6

5

Woodeaton
Wood

Forest Farm

B 4027

1 kilometre

1 mile

WALK 3

Islip

6 miles 10 km
Short cut 5 miles 8 km

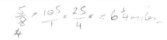

From the ancient village of Islip this walk crosses fields to the hamlet of Noke. It then passes through present day woodland and an area which was once part of the Royal Forest of Shotover to reach Woodeaton, returning to Islip along the river bank.

The going is easy but care is necessary on some stretches of road.

1 SP527139

Start from the car park opposite The Swan Inn next to the River Ray.

Islip has a long history, with evidence of human occupation in the area since the Stone Age. Edward the Confessor was born here in 1004 and the royal link led to a long involvement of the parish with Westminster Abbey, which owned land here for many centuries and is still the patron. At one time the River Ray, a tributary of the Cherwell, was forded here and this is indicated in the origins of the place name which incorporates the Old English name for the river (*Ight*) and a word meaning a place where things are dragged (*Slaep*). The present bridge was completed in 1878. Until 1788, when a turnpike was set up which closed the road

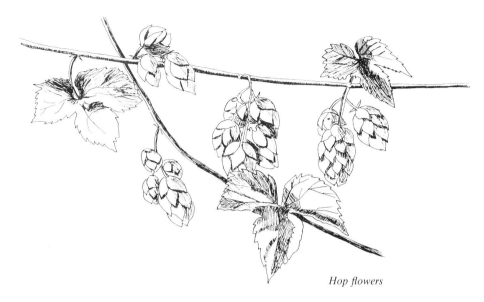

Hop flowers

through the ford, the earlier bridge was only used when the ford was impassable. Flowing west from Otmoor the river was a valuable fishery until it was deepened in the nineteenth century following the Otmoor Drainage Act. A local industry produced osier cages or 'weels' for eel catching.

Cross the bridge walking out of Islip and continue along the road with care.

In the hedgerow grow three closely related plants which, have very different growth forms. Nettles in the base of the hedge can be easily identified, elm has very rough leaves while tendrils of the hop twine round anything they touch. The hop shoots are sensitive to contact and bend in the direction of the touching side, so end up growing round a support. All of these plants can also be seen later along the walk.

When a gate is reached on the left, take the concrete track marked Oxfordshire Way leading through allotments for 10 m, then take a stony track bearing off to the right. Follow this and continue over several stiles along the footpath through arable fields to Noke.

As you walk through these arable fields, notice how there are few or no flowering plants compared to the hedge bottoms and field edges. Herbicide sprays are used to eliminate weeds which would compete with the crop for water, light and space as well as harbouring pests and diseases. Similarly insecticides are used to control aphid infestation of crops which would cause a huge reduction in yield. Aphids suck the sap from the plants and can transmit virus diseases, thus are a serious pest of cereal crops.

From this path there are wide views over the fields and Otmoor. These fields have an interesting past. In Roman times there was a villa and field system here and many centuries later this was Islip's Cow Pasture, probably equivalent to the huge pasture recorded in the Domesday Book of 1086. Even the path is old. There was no burial ground at Noke so in the past this short cut between the two villages was a 'corpse path' as mourners carried the dead to Islip for burial.

Looking to the left, variations in field and hedge pattern can be seen. The hedges crossed by the path are relatively recent, probably planted in the early nineteenth century when the Islip open fields were enclosed. The more sinuous hedge in the distance towards the river marks the line of the parish boundary between Noke and Islip and is much older than the hawthorn enclosure hedges. The hedges are useful refuges for birds and in autumn yellowhammers and flocks of finches can be seen and heard searching for food.

2 SP539131

The path reaches the end of the arable fields. Climb the stile and walk down a grassy track with trees and shrubs on each side. The hedge on your left is part of the parish boundary hedge mentioned above. Look at the mixture of species contained in it and you will see that there is far more variety than in the hedges seen earlier. Look out for a type of hawthorn with

Bumblebee on knapweed

rounded rather than dissected glossy leaves. This is midland or woodland hawthorn and its presence indicates that this hedge is likely to date from a time when this immediate area was woodland. The name Noke means 'at the oak trees' which implies that the settlement started as a clearing within extensive woodland, the remnants of which will be seen later. Notice the increase in numbers of plant species once the intensively cultivated fields are left behind. The succession of flowers in spring – greater stitchwort, cow parsley and ground ivy, followed by white dead nettle, red clover, hogweed, field bindweed and black knapweed – all provide food for numerous bees, flies and other insects.

Continue through a tunnel of hawthorn and blackthorn to the road and turn right. (To visit the thirteenth century church in Noke go left and meet the trail at point 3.) look for a stile in the hedge on the left and follow the footpath along the edge of a field.

The hedge on the left is well cared-for with a thick growth of hawthorn mixed with elm, ash, goat willow and blackthorn. The base provides good cover for small mammals like mice, voles and shrews as well as for the pollinating and predatory insects which are of benefit to agriculture. Rough vegetation at field edges harbours predators of cereal pests, an important factor when considering hedge removal and insecticide spraying.

In summer there may be large carpets of white and pink flowered field bindweed whose twining stems twist round any upright support they contact, like the hops seen earlier.

Continue through the fields until the road is reached.

3 SP546130

At the road turn right and walk past cottages for a quarter of a mile ($\frac{1}{2}$ km). Look out for the remains of an old pond on your right, now a marshy area where

Yellow iris

water cress, yellow iris and willow remain, as well as great willow herb, meadow sweet and water forget-me-not, which can be seen all along this verge. Exposed muddy patches like this are invaluable sources of building material for swallows and house martins.

Continue until a bridleway signed, to Woodeaton, leads off to the right beside a recreation ground and opposite a house called Lower Valley.

This shady path acts as a wildlife corridor through the closely mown recreation ground and agricultural fields. The types of ground plants reflect the lack of sunshine, with fewer small flowering plants than along the roadside verge just passed. Notice, however, that where a gap occurs between the trees, the ground flora becomes more dense and vigorous as well as more varied. See if you can spot paths through the vegetation used by deer, foxes and other animals as they cross between fields and woodland. The plants will be flattened or pushed aside and a whiff of a strong musty odour will show where a fox has recently been. In the spring listen to the birdsong, often quite different to that heard in the fields. Regular songsters in this wooded area are wrens, chaffinch, blue and great tits.

The track soon passes adjacent to Prattle Wood,

Black bryony

the last remnant of woodland which covered this part of Islip parish in the Middle Ages. Over the centuries the woodland has been felled for agriculture and timber, the final clearance taking place in 1806, just before the enclosure of the open fields.

SHORT CUT Keep on along this lane and at the road junction continue straight on to Woodeaton rejoining the trail at the church (section 6)

After about half a mile (1 km), at the third sharp bend in the track, look for a hidden path off to the left which crosses a tiny footbridge. Follow the left-hand hedge for 13 m before continuing across the field to a metal gate.

In late spring stems of black bryony poke through the hedge, yet another species with twining stems. Masses of goosegrass can be seen at the base of the hedge. This too can climb but does so by leaning against other plants and hooking on with hundreds of tiny, stiff, curved hairs that cover the plant.

4 SP543121

At the road turn left and walk with care for a quarter of a mile ($\frac{1}{2}$ km).

This road has seen varied traffic over the centuries. It dates back to at least Roman times, later becoming part of an important route linking Worcester and London (see Walk 1), in use from the time of King Offa in the eighth century. Islip was an important centre for coaches and wagons, with traffic from Buckingham and Bicester also using this route when the Gosford Bridge over the Cherwell was impassable in winter. However, after the building of the Oxford Canal and the improvement of roads in the county as a whole the volume of traffic dropped at the end of the eighteenth century. Now it is busy again with traffic avoiding Oxford and Kidlington but hopefully the extension of the M40 to Birmingham will mean that this ancient route will once again be pleasant to walk along.

Farms like Lower Wood's Farm and Upper Wood's Farm and field names such as Little and Great Forest Grounds, Wood Hill and Wood Plain show the past extent of woodland in the area. The mixed hedges also still contain remnants of the woodland vegetation, species which you will see again off the road.

Just after the triangular road signs, look for a path on the right leading through a small patch of rough land. Cross into the field and follow the path round the right-hand edge of the field soon doubling back on yourself to climb a gentle slope.

Yellow archangel

Notice again the woodland flowers in the hedge bottom, especially obvious in spring when bluebells and yellow archangel are in flower. Look out for the trailing white bryony which climbs by using leaf tendrils which twist tightly round supporting stems. This is quite unrelated to black bryony, but both produce red berries, poisonous to humans but which will be eaten by birds, late in the winter. The traveller's joy or wild clematis in the hedge also climbs by means of tendrils.

Don't miss the place where the path crosses

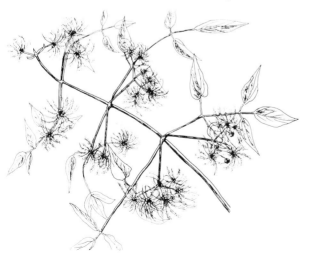

Traveller's joy

through the hedge over a footbridge to continue left
to the edge of a fruit farm.

5 SP544111

At the top of the slope take the path to the right
which meanders through the woodland fringe for a
short distance.

This is Woodeaton Wood and was part of the
Royal Forest of Shotover during the reign of
Henry II (1154 to 1189), as also was the now disappeared woodland referred to earlier, named on a
boundary perambulation of 1298 as Boscus de
Cowaliz. It is possible that the old hedge just followed from the road was part of the 1298 boundary
of the Forest. Royal Forests were composed of a
variety of types of land, not all woodland, although
crops were less important than the provision of
hunting for the King.

The wood contains tall standard oak and ash with
coppice hazel beneath. Coppicing (cutting the trees
back to ground level to encourage new growth) was
a widely used method of woodland management in
the past which provided small wood for fencing,
repairs and fuel, whilst allowing tall standard trees to
reach a suitable size for timber production. Between
the path and the main area of woodland is a bank,
constructed in the distant past to mark the boundary
of the wood with either arable land or woodland in
other ownership.

Leave the wood and continue in the same general
direction along the woodland edge.

The small hill on the right is called Drun's Hill and
remains of a Romano-British iron smelting works
have been found there. It is possible that it supplied
votive objects for a temple which was situated
between here and Islip.

went wrong here Go through a gap in the hedge and down a field
path to the copse in the valley. Turn left at the
bottom of the field in front of Parson's Copse and
follow the path along the field edge to the road. In

the ditch on your right are large tussocks of soft rush whose spiky 'leaves' are really leafless stems which bear clusters of brownish flowers late in the summer.

6 SP535115

found very through deserted pig farm

At the road turn right towards Woodeaton.

The cottage walls often provide sites for nests of various types of solitary bees, especially where the mortar is soft. The nooks and crannies also make a good habitat for plants and mosses.

It is worth pausing to look at the Church of the Holy Rood with its fourteenth century wall-paintings and the small village green beyond with the remains of an old cross and the village pound, used for holding stray animals.

The short cut rejoins here.

Take a stony track to the left off the main road opposite the green and follow this until it reaches a T-junction.

Along the beginning of the path are young elm saplings, easy to identify by the prominent 'wings' on the bark along the branches. Spindle also can be found in the hedgerow with bright pink and orange berries in autumn. It may bear webs containing large numbers of active caterpillars of the small ermine moth. The large buildings on the right were the Manor House, now a school, whilst in the field on the left, ridge and furrow can be seen, especially clear in autumn and winter when the sun is low and the grass short.

7 SP528120

Pause at the junction of the tracks and look left over towards Oxford. On a clear day there is a fine view to the city, the 'dreaming spires' of university colleges contrast with the gleaming white modern block of the John Radcliffe Hospital on the hill. On the wall behind you look for the Ordnance Survey bench mark carved in the stone. This gives a fixed point and height used for surveying.

Turn right along the grassy track and at the end turn left and walk down the field path turning right at the bottom to walk alongside a stream.

This stream is an arm of the River Cherwell. In the tenth century it was called Beetle's water course. The water level fluctuates, so in dry weather it may look no more than a large ditch. The bed is full of reeds and the edge is lined with crack willow, so-called because of its tendency for large branches to fall off the tree. This dangerous habit is curbed if the tree is pollarded like those at Islip so that new growth occurs at the top of the stump, out of reach of grazing animals. These flexible poles were used for making hurdles and also used in hedging. Willow or osier for baskets was grown from twigs set in wet ground and the resulting young growth harvested after two years and then annually for up to thirty years.

The large house visible across the fields on the left is Water Eaton Manor with its dovecote, built in 1586 for Sir Edward Frere. After a time the true river is reached. The flowing water supports a wide variety of wildlife with lush plant growth along the banks and many insects and birds that make good use of this haven in an intensively farmed landscape.

When the path reaches the corner of the field, climb the stile and continue in the same direction as before along the river.

On warm May days, large numbers of mayflies will be seen bobbing over the riverside vegetation. They can be recognised by their two or three 'tails'. Their juvenile stages live for a year or more in the water but the adults emerge from the water, mate and die within a few days – hence their Latin name of *Ephemeroptera*. They can be seen resting on reeds and sedges during their emergence stage. You should also see splendid metallic blue demoiselle

Mayfly at rest

damselflies with large dark patches on their delicate wings. Both pairs of wings are equal in size and shape and when at rest are folded over the body. Related dragonflies have differently shaped wings which are held straight out from the body when at rest.

Continue along the river edge for about half a mile (1 km) and over another stile. The narrow path climbs away from the water's edge but follows the river for a short distance. Turn right along a wire fence, then over a stile and follow a clearly visible path diagonally over the next field to reach allotments situated in an old quarry. The short track leads down to the road, the bridge and the starting point.

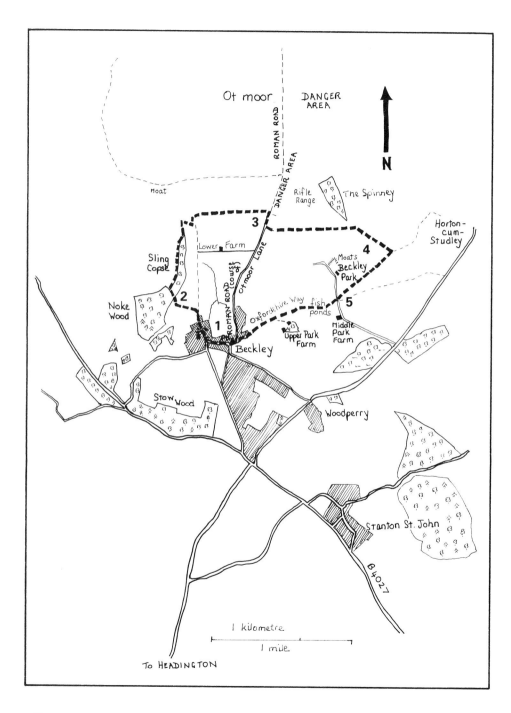

Ot moor

DANGER AREA

ROMAN ROAD

DANGER AREA

N

Moat

Rifle Range

The Spinney

3

Horton-cum-Studley

Lower Farm

Sling Copse

Otmoor Lane

ROMAN ROAD (course)

4

Moats

Beckley Park

2

Noke Wood

Oxfordshire Way

fish ponds

5

1

Beckley

Upper Park Farm

Middle Park Farm

Stow Wood

Woodperry

Stanton St. John

B4027

1 kilometre

1 mile

To HEADINGTON

WALK 4
Beckley
4.5 miles 7 km

This walk leads from the relatively high ground of Beckley village with wide views over Otmoor towards the villages on the far side, down to the edge of the moor following the line of the ancient parish boundary. The return to Beckley passes through an area which was once a medieval deer park. The route provides fairly easy walking over mostly level paths with a short steep climb at the end. Parts may be muddy in wet weather.

1 SP563113

Start in the village of Beckley and take the no-through road, with the church on the left and old cottages on the right.

Beckley is an ancient settlement, possibly dating from before the Romans who were present in this area. There was a villa not far from the Roman road which still crosses Otmoor. It was the most important of the seven Otmoor 'towns' as the lord of Beckley had jurisdiction over the use of the moor. Cattle had to be branded with an iron kept here and the moor pound for stray animals was also in Beckley. As you walk down the lane a good view over the moor can be seen ahead with the church towers of Oddington and Charlton in the distance.

*Lych-gate, Beckley
churchyard*

Take the track at the end of the tarmac road. After a hundred yards climb the stile on the left and follow the footpath leading across the field diagonally left downhill.

This group of fields were once part of Beckley Common, an open area distinct from the common land on Otmoor which would have been used for rough grazing and for gathering fuel. Today it is still grazing land, the fields formed at the time of the Parliamentary Inclosure of Beckley in 1827.

A regular feature of grazed fields is the number of characteristic plants protected from cattle, horses or sheep. Nettles and thistles hurt a soft mouth and docks taste bitter. Creeping thistle and spear thistle are eaten by many insects; the damaged patches and webbing on leaves and the swollen lumps on parts of some stems are signs of this. These thistles have accidentally been introduced to Canada and America where they are now pest plants because there are

Beckley cottages

Greater burnet

no native predators to control them. The flowers are very attractive to bees and butterflies as well as to the bright, reddy-orange 'uniformed', soldier beetles.

Over the next stile, follow the narrow path through scrub on the edge of a rough field.

The wet nature of the bottom field is probably one reason why this land was used as commonland rather than for arable or pasture. It is marked by tussocks of hard rush, a tough plant not eaten much by sheep and cattle; you will see it growing in many grazed fields along this walk, an indication of poor drainage. The grass in this corner has not been improved too much with fertiliser; greater burnet, with unusual dark red, tightly clustered flowerheads, mauve cuckooflower, yellow vetchling and a variety of other flowers grow here. The large patch of yellow daisy-like flowers is flea bane, an aromatic plant which used to be dried and placed in bedding to ward off fleas.

63

2   SP559118

At the bottom of the field the path leads through a strip of old woodland.

On the left is a boundary bank between Noke Wood and Sling Copse on the right, a very good example of typical hazel coppice. Noke Wood was once part of the Royal Forest of Shotover during the reign of Henry II in the twelfth century. In spring many flowers along this path indicate the antiquity of this woodland – yellow archangel, wood anemone, dog's mercury and bluebells. On the bank look out for obvious well-trodden animal paths about twenty cm wide, used probably by deer and foxes. Birds which can be heard include the chiff-chaff calling its name, also wrens, blackcaps, robins and great tits. The woods are silent in summer, following breeding, when the birds are now moulting.

Turn right and walk along the field edge for some distance.

A wide mown grassy path has been left at the edge of this large arable field and thanks to the care taken by the farmer in spraying operations, many flowers

Chiff-chaff

can still be found here, this being particularly obvious in spring. Primroses, bugle, greater stitchwort, violets, celandine and many other flowers scatter the verge and banks of the large ditch alongside. The coppice, visible through the hedge, would in the past have been cut in a regular cycle depending on the size of wood needed for poles and fencing. Regrowth occurs from the base of the tree, the stool, and provides a long-term renewable supply of materials.

A map of Oxfordshire made in 1797 by Richard Davis of Lewknor shows that the area now covered by this huge field was at that time composed of several small fields probably formed by clearing woodland about ten years earlier. The farm visible across the field to the left is Lower Farm but then was called New Farm.

Follow the path over a bridge and continue along a field edge with a ditch on the left.

The wet nature of low-lying Otmoor can be seen in the water-filled ditches. Bright green flote-grass grows in this ditch as well as broader-leaved canary grass, with extra colour in summer from the pink flowers of great willow herb and the dark red of figwort. Hogweed grows in profusion here and its large flowerheads are very attractive to a large number of bright coloured flies, bugs, bees and beetles. Spiders and aphids are frequent residents amongst the hollow, ridged stems supporting the flowerheads.

Over another bridge turn left and then soon right, following the line of an embankment, keeping it on your right-hand side.

This low lying field was part of one of Beckley's two medieval open fields which, by 1580, was divided so that this land became Lower Field, thus giving the village three fields for crop rotation. These survived until 1827 when the land was rearranged by Parliamentary Inclosure.

Notice the dark alluvial soil here which contrasts with the lighter sandy-based soil seen on the higher parts of this walk.

Look out for slender-bodied damselflies resting or flying along this hedgerow. The bright blue azure damselfly can be seen together with the large red damselfly, one of two British red species. This one has black legs, the small red has red legs.

The thick vegetation and scrub on the bank provides shelter and food for all sorts of wildlife, another example of a useful semi-natural corridor within agricultural land.

Continue in the same direction along a stony track towards a metal gate.

Here clumps of large-leaved horse radish can be found. The leaves are a favourite food of snails which, in hot weather, can often be seen glued to them with slime to retain moisture. Notice how the yellow and striped snails are well disguised amongst the upright grass stems.

3 SP570127

Turn right alongside the gate, over a bridge and emerge onto a wide track. Turn right along the track for 200 metres.

This track is part of the Roman road which led across the moor. It was an important north-south route linking the large Roman towns of Towcester on Watling Street (now the A5) to the north with Silcester, situated between Reading and Basingstoke. Oxfordshire Roman settlements along this road were at Dorchester-on-Thames and Alcester, a vanished settlement, north of Otmoor near Bicester and close to the junction with another major route, Akeman Street.

The scrubby vegetation, much of it willow, provides a good home for summer visiting nightingales and if you are lucky you may hear them singing in this area.

At the junction with the road leading left into the Rifle Range take the adjacent path over a stile through hedge trees into a field. The far end of this field is part of a BBONT (Berks, Bucks and Oxon

*Nightingale (above) and
grasshopper warbler
(below)*

Naturalists' Trust) nature reserve but access is limited to permit holders because the range is in frequent use.

The grassland here contains large tussocks of coarse, wet-loving, tufted-hair grass and a variety of unusual flowering plants. One is dyer's greenweed a relative of gorse and broom. Its yellow flowers were used to produce a yellow dye which could be mixed with the blue from woad to produce a green dye, hence its name. This field was known as Park Mede and has probably been grassland for many centuries. Grasshopper warblers are to found in this extensive rough grassland and scrub. You may hear their high-pitched, soft, continuous chirring grasshopper-like song in early summer.

Follow the path in line with the right hand hedge. As you get closer to the brick structure at the end of the range, look out for a stile in the trees on the right and cross over into the adjacent field. Continue in the same direction as before, keeping the hedge on the left and crossing another stile.

These fields show traces of ridge and furrow, which shows that at some time in the past they were cultivated before being turned into pasture. Traces here are not very distinct, the furrows being indicated by lines of rushes which prefer wetter ground than do buttercups which grow mainly on the ridges. Green woodpeckers may be seen hereabouts. One of their favourite types of insect food is ants and they will use their strong, probing beaks to attack ant hills to find them.

When the path reaches the corner of the field, bear right and continue along this side of the field.

The trail is now following the line of part of the old boundary of Beckley Park, the shape of which can still be clearly traced on an Ordnance Survey map. The deer park, first recorded in 1175, was enclosed by a stone wall between 1192 and 1197. In 1229 the manor of Beckley, including the park, was given to Richard, Earl of Cornwall and brother of Henry III. He later stocked the park with deer and

Dyer's green weed

68

had a deer-leap constructed so that deer could enter the park from outside but could not escape. The park continued to have royal associations for several centuries.

Look over the hedge to the left where much more distinct ridge and furrow can be seen. These fields were part of the medieval West Field belonging to Horton which at that time was a hamlet in Beckley parish (see Walk 7). Cultivation took place for longer in these fields, so building up higher ridges than those seen earlier on the land to the right which, at the time of a map made in 1641, was still uncultivated grassland.

4 SP584121

Continue in the same direction into another field. At the corner turn right and again follow the path keeping the hedge on your left.

Hidden in the trees across the field to the right is Beckley Park House. Built originally as a moated hunting lodge in the thirteenth century, it eventually replaced the manor house in the village which was in ruins by the middle of that century. By 1600 the house had been rebuilt and it is this Tudor brick building which still exists. Although now known as Beckley Park House, in the eighteenth century this site was called Lower Park Farm to distinguish it from Middle and Upper Park Farms, all built around the same time. Their names reflect the past use of the land and show that cultivation of the old wood-pasture of the parkland probably only took place from about the beginning of the seventeenth century.

Continue in the same direction over a stile and footbridge to the end of the next field.

Here you can see more examples of ridge and furrow marked by different plants choosing the relatively wetter or drier habitats.

Notice how in this field the direction of the ridges changes showing how large fields were often subdivided into groups of ridges, called furlongs, which were usually named and used for different crops.

5 SP578116

At the kissing gate go straight over the tarred road and continue in the same direction as before, through trees, on a narrow path alongside a deep ditch.

To the left you can see the remains of medieval fishponds where fish were 'farmed' for food. On the slope above the pond area is Middle Park Farm.

Over the stile at the end of the trees, follow the path uphill, skirting round Upper Park Farm.

Once again there are wide views over Otmoor on the right. Look behind you to see in the distance the long ridge of the Chiltern Hills over twenty miles away topped by the Stokenchurch telecommunications tower.

At the top of the hill, climb the stile and cross the field straight ahead to reach the farm track where the trail turns right to return to Beckley.

It was in this area that a Roman villa was found in 1862 with the remains of a mosaic pavement and coloured wall plaster. The site was destroyed the same year and now nothing is visible.

Where the path passes through a thick hedge at the field edge look for remains of the stone wall built 700 years ago to enclose Beckley Park.

Follow the track down to the village and back to the start.

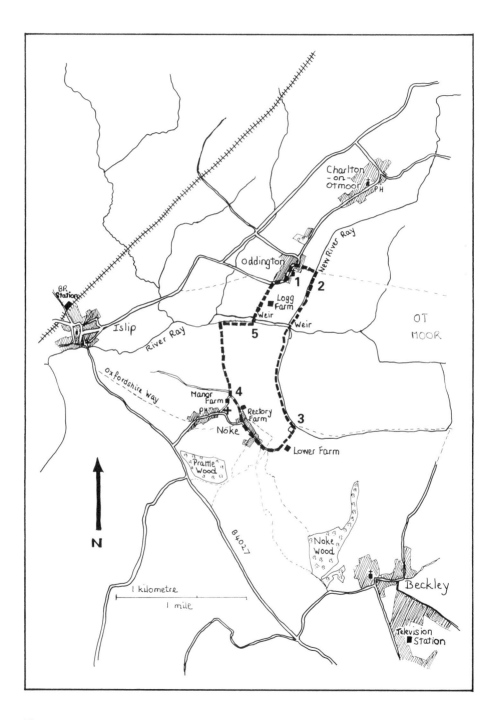

Charlton
-on-
Otmoor
PH

New River Ray

Oddington

1

2

Logg
Farm

Weir

Weir

5

OT
MOOR

BR.
Station

Islip

River Ray

Oxfordshire Way

Manor
Farm

4

PH

Rectory
Farm

3

Noke

Lower Farm

Prattle
Wood

N

B4027

Noke
Wood

Beckley

1 kilometre

1 mile

Television
Station

WALK 5
Oddington
4.75 miles 8 km

This walk explores the western side of Otmoor, following part of the New River Ray and the line of the main perimeter drainage ditch. On the way back to Oddington the trail passes through Noke and follows the banks of the old River Ray.

1   SP554148

Start in Oddington and take the stony track which leads off the small green, down towards the river.

Like Charlton, Oddington is built on an outcrop of cornbrash rock which raises the village twelve feet (four metres), above the plain of Otmoor. The name means Otta's hill, presumably the same Otta who gave his name to Otmoor itself. The settlement dates from the sixth century and a pagan cemetery has been found in the Rectory garden. Over the hedge to the right a pattern of bumps and hollows can be seen. The hollows and platforms mark the long since vanished sites of village houses, and show that the present village has reduced in extent over the centuries. The Manor House, which was pulled down in 1800, was also situated in this field. In the past Oddington was famous for its springs whose minerals were reputed to cure cattle of the 'Otmoor evil'.

New River Ray

The path is lined with nettles, woundwort, and much cow-parsley with its tiny white flowers held in a flat flowerhead called an umbel. Once the petals fall from the flowerhead, the seeds will begin to swell very quickly even though many branches of the plant have still to flower: seed production is concentrated on the first flowering umbels at the top of the plant and the end of the branches. As the seeds set, so the plant dies back, shaded out by other plants around it. You will see many plants which carry their flowers in flat umbels; hogweed, angelica, wild carrot and parsnip, all flowering at different times of the year. The path soon reaches a bridge over the New River Ray, a product of the 1815 inclosure of Otmoor (see Introduction).

This is a good spot to look at the water plants. Some have their roots under water but their leaves above the surface. This allows the leaves to take in oxygen and pass it to the roots so that they do not drown. Floating waterlily leaves have lots of holes (stomata) on the top of the leaves to take in air. Most land plants have these on the underside of their leaves to regulate water loss or transpiration which also takes place through the stomata. Plants which are completely submerged are, like fish, very efficient in extracting oxygen from the water.

2 SP555147

Over the bridge turn right and follow the line of the New River Ray for half a mile (1 km).

As you walk notice how the vegetation growing on each side of the track is different. On the left are lush grasses, nettles, tall hogweed and thistles, whilst on the right the grass is more sparse with lots of flowering plants; yellow rattle, agrimony, vetches, black medick and meadow buttercup. This variation may be due to a number of factors such as soil disturbance or shading. The flowers on both sides are good sources of nectar for butterflies and bees. The tall hedges provide good nesting sites for many birds and the proximity of water means that there will be plenty of insect food for them.

On the right glimpses of the water can be seen while, through gaps in the hedge on the left, there are views of Otmoor, its open wind-swept expanse contrasting with the sheltered conditions along this enclosed path.

By a farm bridge look over towards Oddington and the bumps and hollows of the deserted part of the village will be seen again, especially clearly in a dry summer or with a light snow or frost cover.

Continue along the track and cross the small weir as the path crosses the old River Ray. The old and the new branches of the river meet further down stream between here and Islip but run parallel for a time. The New River was dug and the flow of water diverted from the original course in an attempt to drain the low-lying, frequently flooded, Otmoor plain. Land-owners hoped to make their fortunes after the common land of Otmoor was enclosed in 1815, however, this was not to be. In most places the ground is still not well drained and productivity has remained low except where modern pumping equipment has substantially lowered the water table.

Notice some of the wildlife in the watercourses. The floating duckweed has three round leaflets and a single root which dangles into the water. The leaflets easily break apart and each can then form a new plant which is how this tiny plant spreads over the water so quickly. In winter some of the leaflets sink to the bottom to avoid flooding and freezing. Small sparrow-sized brown sedge warblers sing amongst the tall rushes. The males often fly, singing ten-twenty feet into the air and then drop again as part of their territorial and courtship displays. Damsel-flies, mayflies, stoneflies and caddis flies all may be seen here as their larval stages all live in water. Notice how the wings of all these insects have a complicated network of veins on them. This is a 'primitive' character found in many, very old fossil insects whereas bees, butterflies and beetles only

Goat's beard seed head

Teasel flower head

have a few parallel lines of veins on their wings, an 'advanced' feature.

At a slight bend in the track continue along the grassy track. At a metal gate carry on in the same direction along the closely mown grassy path.

Much of the track from Oddington follows the line of a 'greenway' which has been in use from at least the thirteenth century although when its route was defined in the 1815 Inclosure Award it was slightly altered near Oddington.

The fields have changed from damp pasture and rough grazing for cattle to arable as a result of modern drainage, installed about twenty-five years ago. You may see sheep grazing in fields which in the past, especially in winter, would have been far too wet because of the danger of liver fluke, a parasitic infection carried by water snails. The high banks to the ditches stop the water flowing back onto the land in winter.

Although surrounded by intensively farmed land these banks and ditches provide a good habitat for wild plants. Those growing on the dry banks are quite different to those in the wet ditch which contains sedges, rushes, yellow iris or flag, reed mace and meadow sweet with clusters of creamy white flowers. The flowers were once added to drinks to give a sweet taste and the common name could be a corruption of the Anglo-Saxon word meaning honey-herb. The green slimy growth which can be seen most frequently in autumn or winter in some of the ditches is *Spirogyra*, an alga, which grows in profusion in water made nutrient-rich by agricultural fertilizer washing off the fields. On the banks look for purple flowered vetches, clover and goat's beard whose short-lived yellow flowers are only open for a morning, hence the other name of Jack-go-to-bed-at-noon. They produce huge, strong, dandelion-like seed heads.

Teasels can be found on both damp and dry parts of the ditch. Goldfinches and other birds are attracted by the seeds held in the prickly fruiting heads.

77

The dry brush-like seed heads were used in the past in the production of woollen cloth, first to card the wool by teasing the fibres into alignment prior to spinning and then to comb and raise the nap of the woven cloth. The name teasel comes from the Anglo-Saxon *taesan* meaning to tease. The paired leaves form a cup round the stem and often contain water which can prove a death trap to unwary insects, although teasel is not an insect eating plant.

Tandem of red damsel flies

The high bank gives a good vantage point for the surrounding countryside seen at closer quarters on other walks in this book. To the right is the hamlet of Noke with further to the right on the skyline the church tower at Islip. The woodland to the right is Prattle Wood and that in front is Noke Wood (see Walks 3 and 4). These ancient landscape features contrast with the modern landmark of the television mast ahead of you on the hill top at Beckley. This quiet area was one of the proposed routes for the M40 which now lies just to the north of Otmoor beyond Fencott and Murcott.

3 SP553130

At the next junction turn right down a farm track from Otmoor to Lower Farm, Noke.

The large pond near the junction is actually a balancing reservoir built to accommodate excess water from the drainage system. It acts as a useful habitat for plants and insects and the island provides a safe nesting site for water-fowl out of reach of foxes. In spring many damsel flies can be seen along the path near the pond. Look out for mating pairs called tandems. After mating the male grips the female behind the head with claspers at the end of his body and carries her around, guarding her until the eggs are laid, thus ensuring that no other male can mate with her. In spring, water plantain (no relation to other plantains) is conspicuous by its large leaves and later by the tall delicate sprays of white flowers, the dead and dry remains of which can

Water plantain

be seen in late autumn as a golden-brown tracery at the edge of the pond.

Go past Lower Farm and continue right along the lane to Noke.

On a map of Oxfordshire made in 1797 Lower Farm was called New Farm, as only within the few preceeding years had a large part of Noke Wood been cleared and enclosed for agricultural land. The settlement of Noke dates probably from late Anglo-Saxon times when it was likely to have been a clearing in extensive woodland. In the sixteenth century it was used as a refuge for members of the University in Oxford who came here to escape the ravages of the plague.

Walk along the road and at a sharp bend bear slightly right down a bridleway next to Rectory Cottage, keeping the old buildings of Rectory Farm on your right. Notice the steeply pitched roof of one of the barns showing that originally it was thatched, the sharp angle of the roof helping the rapid drainage of rain water.

4   SP545133

Continue past Manor Farm on your left and at a junction take the right-hand track, an old lane which led out from the village to the open field called Common or Town Field in the sixteenth century.

In June the hedgerows are full of purple flowered vetches. These complicated pea-like flowers need bumble bee pollinators which are heavy enough to spring apart the petals to reach the nectar and pollen within. Notice that the bumble bees seen here are a different species to the stripy ones found in town gardens. This one has a pale-brown stripe and is known as the buff-tailed bumble bee.

Continue in the same direction along the field edge at the end of the track keeping the hedge on your right.

It is easy to see here how intensive agricultural

activities can reduce wildlife in hedge-bottoms and field edges.

Continue until you reach the old River Ray, now no more than a stream. Turn right and follow the banks of the river to a footbridge.

The land alongside the river was originally lot-meadows. Each year villagers would draw lots for strips of these fields and for the hay which would be harvested from them.

The river banks are lined with pussy willow, attractive throughout the year with silver fluffy catkins in the spring and yellow autumn leaf colours. A member of the same family as crack willow (see Islip and Rycote walks) it is also known as sallow or goat willow. The leathery leaves are rounded in shape, quite different to the long narrow leaves of crack willow. This area of thicket with rough grass-land beyond is a good habitat for mice and voles which in turn are preyed upon by kestrels. You may see some hovering over the area. When the grass is too long they cannot hunt, hence their frequent sightings over the relatively short grass of motorway verges.

5 SP544142

At the footbridge turn left and cross this and the next bridge over the New River Ray.

It is easy to see that the volume of water in the New River is much greater than that in the old river; the water which used to flood Otmoor is now carried in a wide straight channel.

Continue straight on and cross the field to a track. Turn right until Logg Farm is in sight. Take the path off to the left at the side of a paddock, following the edge of the field. When you reach the farm road bear left between the avenue of trees and carry on to the main road.

Look to the right along the farm road and you will see pronounced ridge-and-furrow, more remnants of old open field cultivation. Horse chestnut trees line

*Preaching cross, Oddington
churchyard*

the road; their name comes from the early use of the nuts as feedstuff and the horse-shoe shaped scar that is left after the leaves have fallen. This species was an introduction to Britain, apparently brought here by the Romans.

At the road turn right and return to Oddington.

From the churchyard in Oddington it is possible to see, amongst the hollows and platforms, the line of the track which was part of the greenway followed earlier around the edge of Otmoor to Noke. This part fell into disuse after the formation of the new River Ray and the definition of the present path by the Otmoor Inclosure Award. Look out for the tomb of a Maori princess in the churchyard and for the remains of an old preaching cross.

As the road bends to the right, notice the Victorian letterbox set into the wall.

Follow the road back to the start.

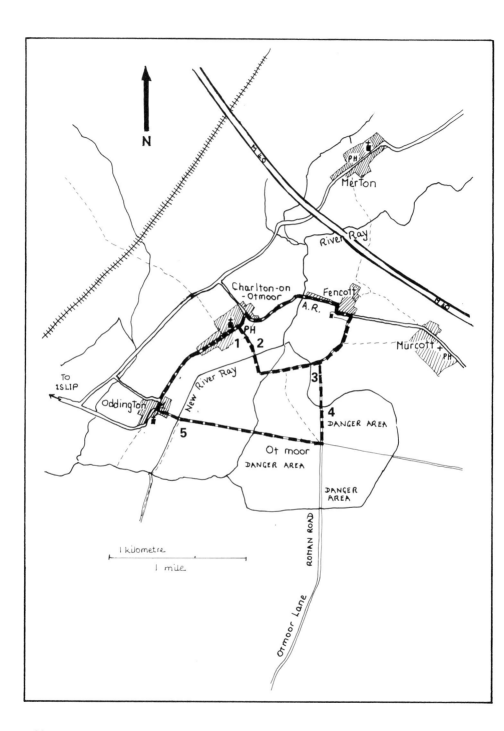

N

Merton

PH

River Ray

M 40

Charlton-on
-Otmoor

Fencott

A.R.

PH

1

2

Murcott +
PH

TO
ISLIP

New River Ray

3

Oddington

4

DANGER AREA

5

Ot moor
DANGER AREA

DANGER
AREA

ROMAN ROAD

Ormoor Lane

1 kilometre

1 mile

WALK 6

Charlton-on-Otmoor

3.5 miles 6 km

Alternative route 3 miles 5 km

This walk takes you on to Otmoor itself. From Charlton the trail leads to the edge of the moor then follows a long section of the route of the Roman road before returning via Oddington. The central part of the walk passes through a MOD rifle range and, unfortunately, when the red flag is flying there is no public right-of-way. If this is the case you can return via Fencott (see alternative route). There is an information board at point four which gives details of the regulations. Muddy in wet weather.

1 SP563178

In Charlton-on-Otmoor look for The Crown opposite the church and take the track to the left of the pub, Otmoor Lane, and follow it downhill.

Charlton has a long history of independence. Its name means 'the settlement of the freemen' and it has never owed allegiance to a lord of the manor. The Crown was the centre for the resistance movement in the 1830s against the enclosure and drainage of Otmoor. Charlton men would meet there, especially on moonlit nights, before going out on to the moor with blackened faces or in other disguises, to break down fences, bridges and ditches. The village did not rely just on agriculture for its livelihood but was a centre for wagon making, quarrying and brickmaking, utilising the outcrop of Cornbrash on which it is built.

On the high wall to the left look for a plant which is a close relative of stinging nettle, pellitory-of-the-wall. It flowers from June to September with greenish blossoms. The young stamens curve inwards but if touched when ripe they scatter a cloud of pollen as they spring outwards. The strange name is derived from the Latin word for wall so really the name means wall-of-the-wall.

On the other side of the track the wall is covered with ivy. The growing stems have the typical five-pointed ivy leaves but notice how the leaves on the flowering shoots often take a different shape and become longer and less lobed. The reason for this change in growth form is uncertain.

This is an old track leading to Otmoor but the hedge was probably planted after the enclosure of Otmoor in the 1830s when the route of the track was straightened. The moor common land extended as far as the outskirts of Charlton; the bend in the road marks the line of the parish boundary and probably where the alteration in alignment started.

2 SP564155

The track leads over a concrete bridge crossing the New River Ray. The man-made origin of the river is obvious with its straight course and regular banks (see Walk 5). Nevertheless it now forms a valuable aquatic habitat for plants and animal life. A plant which can be seen from the bridge is arrowhead. The submerged leaves are long and narrow, those on the water surface are round but those emerging from the water have the arrowhead shape which gives the plant its name. Fast-growing duckweed makes a

Arrowhead

Pond sedge

bright green covering on the slow moving water. In Israel, where dry conditions mean that fodder is scarce for cattle, it is being grown experimentally in tanks because it produces such a large quantity of food material so quickly.

Continue straight on along a rough track until you reach a corrugated iron barn. Turn left here along a rutted track hedged on both sides.

This is another 'new' track, laid out as a result of the enclosure of Otmoor. A footpath which leaves the track on the right over a small stile probably marks the approximate line of the original route from Charlton across the moor to Beckley or Horton.

Along the track look carefully at the plants grow-

Tufted vetch

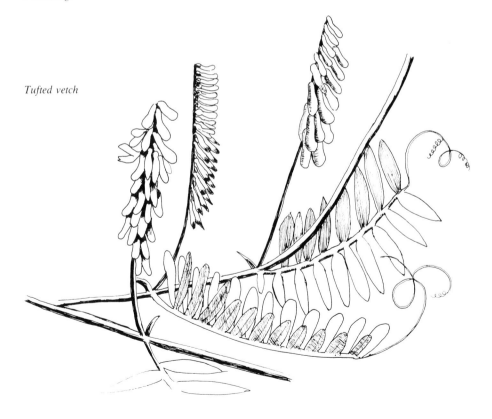

ing there. See if you can distinguish between sedges and grasses. Superficially sedges are similar to grasses but grow predominantly in damp hollows. If you feel the base of the leafy shoots, three sharp ridges, giving a triangular shape to the stem indicate a sedge, while grasses are usually round and smooth. They can often be quite sharp so take care when handling them. The flower heads often have a cluster of brown male flowers at the tip with greenish female flowers grouped below.

Skipper butterfly

You will notice that some plants such as great willowherb and meadow sweet grow only in damper areas at the ditch side, while others prefer the drier ground of the path itself. Where damage can occur from trampling the plants are predominantly grasses which can withstand the wear and tear.

On a sunny summer day there will be several butterflies to spot, all of which have caterpillars which feed on grasses. Look out for meadow brown, marbled white, small heath and large skipper with its triangular outline. Common blues feed on bird's foot trefoil and other members of the pea family, like the tufted vetch, with large clusters of blue flowers which grows in profusion along this part of the track.

3 SP572154

At a junction of tracks, turn right and continue for about half a mile (nearly 1 km). This is the route of the Roman road linking Dorchester and Alcester, an important Roman town and military base situated to the east of Wendlebury north of here. In the 19th century the road was described as being visible as a ridge in the central part of Otmoor with conspicuous amounts of stone present in the muddy lane. It would have been constructed on an embankment or agger using locally quarried stone which ever since has been used by the local inhabitants; early this century people were still extracting the stones which were about a foot below ground level.

The fields on each side of the track were formed

after the enclosure of Otmoor. Although the instigators of the drainage and enclosure of Otmoor had high hopes of rich arable crops, as you can see, most of the fields even today are only used for rough grazing and some hay production. Fields which can be seen on Walk 5 are now productive but only after much recent intensive drainage.

As you walk, it is interesting to compare the abundance and variety of the plants growing along the track with the appearance of the grazed pasture. Most flowering plants cannot tolerate grazing, only low-growing or protected plants like bitter-tasting buttercups or tough rushes survive. Some fields have been ploughed and reseeded with fast-growing grasses. Flowering plants are absent here as well, this time because the new grasses crowd them out. In contrast the verges have luxuriant vegetation in summer with yellow vetchling, the creamy heads of meadow sweet and bright yellow flags or iris in the damper patches.

4 SP572147

At this point you will reach the MOD notice board. Look ahead to see if the red flag is flying. If so, you should turn back and follow the alternative route (see below). If the red flag is not flying, continue straight on to the end of the track and turn right down another track again hedged on both sides.

This lane was defined in the Otmoor Inclosure Award but it is difficult to tell whether or not it follows the line of the original route from Oddington across the moor to Horton.

The sheltered track lined with hawthorn, sloes and willows is very different from the open expanse of the moor which would have been here before about 1830. Only the underlying, wet nature of the ground remains, shown by horsetails, great willow herb and meadow sweet, all indicators of damp conditions. Sedges occur in the wetter hollows in the path; several different sorts grow along the path, see if you can find some.

Other plants can also be found which attract butterflies like green-veined white and comma, the latter can be identified by the uneven wing shape and a white 'comma' on the underwing. Their caterpillars feed on different plants; the green-veined white lives on charlock and similar plants while the comma makes use of three, closely related plants with dissimilar appearances, namely, hops, elm and nettles (see Walk 3). Other caterpillars are grass feeders but the short vegetation in nearby fields is not suitable for them.

As you walk, look across the fields on your right. Through gaps in the hedge the church tower of St Mary the Virgin at Charlton is easily visible on the low ridge on which the village is situated. In the past a curfew was rung from this church during the winter and this helped to guide travellers across the wet misty wastes of Otmoor.

After a time you will cross what looks like a large farm ditch. This in fact is the old River Ray which now gains its water from the ditches draining this side of Otmoor. The main flow of water was diverted along the New River Ray in the 1830s.

In autumn the hedges are colourful with red fruits of hawthorn and rose, haws and hips, as well as the purple of sloes. The red based colours are very visible to birds and animals which are especially sensitive to this part of the light spectrum thus finding their food easily. In turn the seeds within the fruits will be dispersed by the feeding birds and animals. Large flocks of wintering fieldfares and redwings descend on these trees in winter and can strip them bare in a matter of minutes.

The common shrubs within the hedge, namely hawthorn and blackthorn or sloe, have names which date back to Anglo-Saxon times. The name hawthorn means 'hedge thorn' and has evolved from the same word root as hedge-row, an indication of the long use of this shrub as an effective barrier. Sloe comes from Anglo-Saxon words close in meaning to the verb 'to strike', perhaps because the wood was used in the past for making flails, for beating the grain from corn ears.

5 SP556148

At the end of the track carry on over the bridge crossing the New River Ray and walk up the stony track to Oddington (see Walk 5). Turn right at the road and follow it back to Charlton.

The fields in Oddington were enclosed in 1791 and the ones on the right were probably meadow with the arable land further away from Otmoor where conditions were drier. Further along the road past the telephone exchange, the land on the right was called Lammas Land which meant that it was subject to strict traditional rules of grazing dating back to medieval times or even earlier. The name of Lammas was originally given to 1st August, traditionally harvest festival, from Old English, 'loaf Mass'. Grazing was allowed probably for the animals of specific villagers on Lammas Land from August to February and then the land shut up to allow the hay to grow. When this practice died out here is uncertain, probably during the last century after the inclosure of Charlton in 1858, the last of the seven Otmoor 'towns'. In late summer look out for oak trees along the route. At this time of the season they produce new growth of small bright green shoots called Lammas growth.

The road is slightly higher than the moor and the saucer shape of Otmoor can be seen quite clearly; with the coral and sand hills around Beckley, the sponge reef of Horton and beyond, and the cornbrash limestone ridge of Oddington and Charlton in front forming the boundaries (see Introduction).

Soon the road reaches Charlton and the starting point. It is interesting to see how many cottage names commemorate previous trades and occupations.

ALTERNATIVE ROUTE

If the red flag is flying, retrace your steps back along the Roman road to the junction met earlier and fork right.

This is another track which was probably realigned when Otmoor was enclosed and leads to Fencott and Murcott. The moor stretched right to the edges of these hamlets which are still very small and as their names imply were prone to flooding in the past. In the fifteenth century there was a causeway between the two villages but the present road was made after the enclosure of the open fields in 1849.

When you reach the road turn left. (If you want to see Murcott, where there is a pub, turn right.)

The original road linking the hamlets with Charlton was called Church Way; as neither hamlet had a church the villagers had to go to Charlton. This was often flooded in wet weather when the river overflowed. The route of the Roman road crosses the modern road just before the bridge and it is interesting to note that one of the old field names in the vicinity was Street Hill, a reference to the ancient road. The river here is the Ray, seen in its original state before its diversion into the new river, a little further downstream.

Continue back to Charlton and the start of the walk.

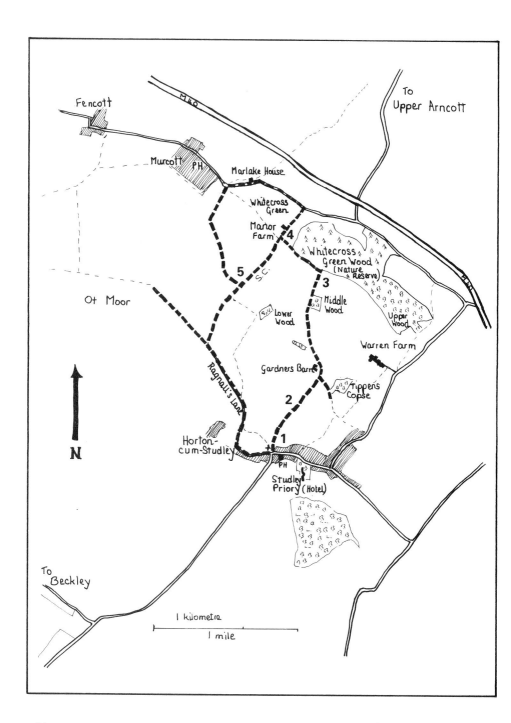

Fencott

To
Upper Arncott

M40

Murcott PH

Marlake House

Whitecross
Green

Manor
Farm

4

Whitecross
Green Wood
(Nature
Reserve)

S.C.

5

Ot Moor

Lower
Wood

Middle
Wood

Upper
Wood

3

Warren Farm

Gardners Barn

Ragnall's Lane

Tippens
Copse

2

Horton-
cum-Studley

1

PH

Studley
Priory (Hotel)

N

To
Beckley

1 kilometre

1 mile

Horton-cum-Studley

5 miles 8 km
Short cut 4 miles 6.5 km

This walk leads through an area which until the early nineteenth century was part of Beckley parish. It follows old tracks, past a deserted village site and ancient woodland returning to Horton along the edge of Otmoor. Parts of this walk can be sticky in wet weather.

1 SP594124

Start in Horton beside St Barnabas Church and take Mill Lane past some modern houses. Continue along the wide grassy lane with thick hedges on each side.

Horton was originally an important hamlet in the parish of Beckley and for many centuries had a larger population and greater prosperity, probably because of the richer more productive soil here compared with the thinner sandy soil at Beckley. Beckley is the older settlement, Horton probably arising as woodland was cleared (see Walk 4). Its name means muddy or dirty town. The ground underfoot is clay, especially noticeable if the weather is wet. Although only about thirty metres above Otmoor, the ridge to the right is a prominent feature. It is composed of Arngrove stone formed from the fossilised remains of sponges which rests directly upon the Oxford Clay. Look out for fragments of these fossils in the fields as you walk.

Studley was another hamlet of Beckley parish formed when the priory, founded in about 1176, acquired most of the land you will walk through for the next mile or so. In the past this field was called Mill Field, as Studley windmill was situated on the high ground. The bumps in the field are probably remnants of ridge-and-furrow cultivation.

The hedges lining the track contain several shrub species, an indication that they are probably older than the hawthorn hedges planted in the nineteenth century. A rough rule of thumb is that each shrub species present in a thirty yard stretch of hedge represents one hundred years in the age of the hedge but this has to be taken in conjunction with documentary and other plant evidence. If, for example, the hedges were left as remnants of cleared woodland then the mix of shrubs present might imply that the hedge is older than is actually the case.

The absence of big tussocks of grass indicates that this track is regularly mown. One plant growing here which tolerates this is white dead nettle its non-stinging leaves look similar to stinging nettle, hence the name 'dead'. It flowers almost all year but peaks in spring and is a valuable food source for bumble bees. Another white, spring and summer flower is cow parsley; its bright green feathery leaves start to grow in autumn and winter, an optimistic foretaste of the warmer seasons to come.

2   SP598129

At the end of the track follow the path along the field edge and then over a bridge into the next field. Continue straight on across the field to emerge on to a track close to Gardner's Barn. For a good view

Burnet moth on self-heal

over Otmoor, turn right uphill for a short distance. From this vantage point you can see the large expanse of Otmoor's rough grassland looking very different from the bright green cultivated fields in the foreground. Most of these fields have been formed by amalgamating smaller old fields, a process which started about two hundred and fifty years ago and is still continuing. If you look carefully you can see a ridge across the field you have just walked across, showing where a hedge used to be until quite recently. As you face Otmoor look slightly to the right beyond the buildings below. The three irregular shaped brownish fields you can see were originally common land called Asham Marsh, used for pasture by villagers of the seven Otmoor towns and now a BBONT nature reserve. The regular fields to the left beyond the grassy track just walked along were likely to have been formed by the enclosure of the open fields during the early part of the nineteenth century.

Retrace your steps and follow the track past Gardner's Barn. This area was once a settlement called Ash or Nash. It was in existence at the time of the Domesday Book but when Studley Priory took over the manor of Ash, the village ceased to be inhabited from the end of the twelfth century. Now its presence is only remembered in field names like Asham Mead, Asham Field and Nash Field.

On the bank to the right look for the purple flowers of self-heal, a low-growing plant which, as its name suggests, has medicinal properties useful in the treatment of sore throats and tonsilitis. At the end of this track a group of trees have been planted in the field corner on the right. This future small woodland will enhance the landscape and provide shelter and food for wildlife. Birds and small mammals such as voles, mice and shrews frequent these islands of natural vegetation amongst the cultivated land. In the case of shrews, this cover is vital as their high rate of metabolism means they have to feed throughout the day and so would be vulnerable to predators without it.

Common shrew

Follow the track left past a newly planted hedge on your left and look out for a footpath sign pointing across the unhedged field on your right. Take the path which heads towards the patch of woodland.

At the edge of the arable field look for a variety of 'weeds of cultivation'. These are species which regularly occur in soil disturbed or ploughed, needing the open ground so produced. On undisturbed ground they are soon outgrown by larger plants and grasses. They make the most of short-term open conditions by growing quickly and producing flowers and seeds when quite small. Round-leaved geranium, field speedwell and groundsel are all examples of these.

Follow the path keeping the woodland and then the hedge on your right. The Oxfordshire Agricultural Education Centre at Warren Farm can be seen on the hilltop to the right. Here the interaction between modern farming and wildlife may be studied by school classes with the aid of a nature trail which uses this path. (Contact the School Liaison Officer Tel. 086 735 794.)

3   SP598144

When you reach the field corner with Whitecross Green Wood in front of you turn left and follow the outside of the wood.

This woodland was originally called Priors Wood and is likely to be the woodland described in the Domesday Book as 'wood for 200 swine' which belonged to Ash. It later belonged to Studley Priory, hence the old name, and part was within the Royal Forest of Bernwood (see Walk 8). Today Whitecross Green Wood is a nature reserve owned and managed by BBONT who aim to gradually replace the conifers, planted by the Forestry Commission in the mid 1960's, with the broad-leaved species which originally grew here; the antiquity of the wood is shown by its rich woodland flora.

Some deciduous trees and shrubs such as oak, hazel, willow and blackthorn line the edges of the conifer blocks. Their varied shapes and leaf colours contrast with the dark rows of conifers. Grasses and flowers can grow beneath deciduous trees as it is lighter here, but the darkness within the plantation eliminates ground plants. All the deciduous trees produce their flowers before their leaves open so that the wind can blow the pollen about to ensure fertilisation of the female flowers. Willow is an exception as it relies on early spring insects to pollinate the flowers. Hazel catkins are formed by late summer but only open in late winter when the weather begins to warm. Notice how different trees of the same species flower at different times so that not all will be harmed by sudden frosts.

There is public access along the rides only but no dogs are allowed.

Muntjac deer can be seen in the vicinity of the wood. These dog-sized deer from China were introduced at the turn of the century into deer parks from which they have escaped and spread throughout south-east England. As they nibble tree seedlings, new plantings have to be protected by plastic tubes.

Muntjac deer

All along the wood edge, paths made by deer and other animals can be seen leading to and from the wood. The deer graze at the field edge and in soft mud their two-toed footprints are numerous. Sheep and cattle also have two toes but horses have only one toe which forms the hoof.

Follow the edge of the wood and look out for a stile through the hedge just past the end of the woodland. Cross over this and continue to the end of the field where another stile leads onto a track.

4 SP595148

Turn right along the track.

SHORT CUT Turn left here and rejoin the walk at point 5.

The track leads past Manor Farm and Whitecross Green Farm which, like the wood, gets its name from a piece of old common land which belonged to yet another hamlet called Marlake. Many of the original fields here were gained by assarting (clearing) land from Otmoor and Bernwood.

At the road, turn left and walk for half a mile (1 km).

Marlake House on the right was a pub until about fifty years ago and the name is all that remains of the old hamlet.

Continue until you reach a chapel on the right where you take the grassy track opposite on the left beside a wide drainage ditch. Follow the track for a short distance then soon climb a stile and follow the field edge and path right to a track. Turn right and then immediately left once through the gateway. Continue along the edge of this field alongside a broad wet ditch until a junction is reached.

Notice how the vegetation here is different to that seen at the beginning of the walk. Many coarse leaved sedges are found among the grasses, recognisable by their triangular stems, most easily seen and felt at their bases. In the ditch the wet conditions are ideal for plants like great willow herb and common reed. Reeds last through the winter with hard cane-like stems and fluffy flower heads which make good nest material for hedgerow birds, while the small seeds are a good food source. In the Norfolk fens reeds were traditionally used for thatching material and may possibly have been used in the Otmoor area in the distant past as they would have been much more plentiful before drainage took place. In the hedgerow remains of old elm stumps felled after Dutch elm disease suggest how different the landscape must have looked less than twenty years ago with many more hedgerow trees.

For some distance the path follows the line of the parish boundary, once that between Beckley and Otmoor, now between Horton-cum-Studley and Fencott and Murcott. Otmoor was never technically within a parish but was extra-parochial common land used by villagers from the seven towns.

5 SP590143

At the junction the short cut rejoins the main walk. Turn right at the junction (straight on for those who took the short cut).

The field to the left is another part of Asham Marsh mentioned earlier. It figured in a dispute in the sixteenth century when neighbouring land owners declared a right to inclose it. A royal enquiry at Beckley decided that the villagers had rights of common pasture over the land, and inclosure did not take place until the nineteenth century. Now a nature reserve it contains a variety of grasses and flowering plants such as great burnet, devil's bit scabious and dyer's green weed which all like wet conditions. Devil's bit scabious is so named because of its short root; an old story tells how once this plant had a long root which could cure many diseases, but the devil, in envy, bit it off. A footpath leads through part of the reserve; pause here for a closer look before rejoining the main walk.

The path continues alongside a high embankment to a track where you turn left.

For a longer walk turn right here, along the grassy track towards Otmoor. This track is very attractive in summer with many flowers and insects to be seen, but you will have to return to this point to continue the main walk. As you walk up the track back towards Horton you will see grassy fields with marked ridge-and-furrow remains. The fields on each side of the track were once the large open fields of Horton. Originally just one huge area divided into furlongs, by the thirteenth century there were three fields here, with four by the late sixteenth century. In the eighteenth century each field was cultivated in a rotation of two years of crops followed by a year of fallow when nothing was grown. Crops included wheat, rye, peas and oats. The open fields were inclosed by Act of Parliament in 1827. This track to Horton was once a narrow strip of common land called Harrow Marsh leading off the moor to the village.

When you reach the road junction turn left. The land on the left in the angle of the lane was

Devil's bit scabious

originally in the form of small fields or closes, which by 1786 amounted to about 150 acres near the village. These were let to tenants by the land owner, Lord Abingdon.

Return to your start near the Victorian church.

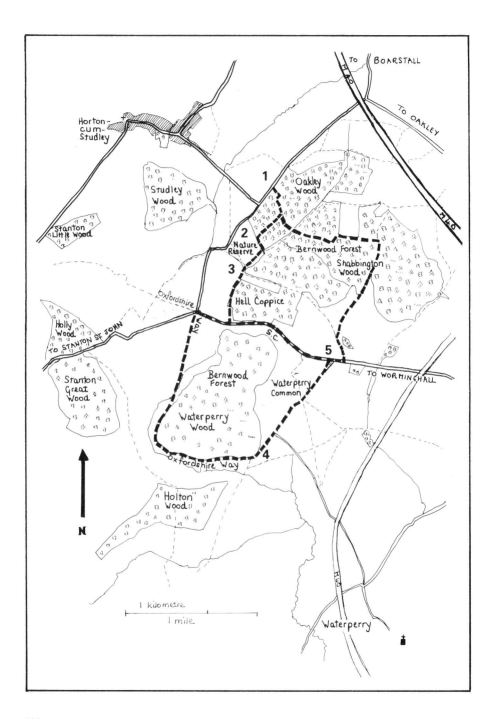

TO BOARSTALL

TO OAKLEY

Horton-cum-Studley

Studley Wood

Stanton Little Wood

1

Oakley Wood

2

Nature Reserve

Bernwood Forest

Shabbington Wood

3

Hell Coppice

Oxfordshire

Holly Wood

TO STANTON St JOHN

Stanton Great Wood

K.K.

S.C.

5

Bernwood Forest

Waterperry Wood

Waterperry Common

TO WORMINGHALL

4

Oxfordshire Way

N

Holton Wood

1 kilometre

1 mile

Waterperry

106

WALK 8

Bernwood

6.25 miles 10 km
Short cut 4.25 miles 7 km

This walk passes through part of Bernwood Forest, much of which is now a Forestry Nature Reserve managed in conjunction with English Nature and is one of the richest butterfly sites in the country. Following the Oxfordshire Way around the edge of Waterperry Wood, a pleasant country walk can be enjoyed through an area which for a time was considered as the route for the M40.

1 SP611117

Start from the carpark on the Oakley to Horton-cum-Studley road. From the information board at the start of the butterfly trail follow the signed paths through woodland, turning left at the wide gravel track. At the first junction turn right down the grassy track.

Notice how the corners of the junctions and edges of the tracks or rides through the forest are carefully managed so that grass is less dominant and flowering plants are encouraged. Mowing is done on a several year cycle so that the differing heights and thickness of the vegetation provide a variety of habitats for different butterfly species. After mowing, the cuttings are removed to ensure that the soil does not

Pearl-bordered fritillary

become too rich, so preventing the grasses from crowding out flowering plants. Plants like violets and devil's bit scabious are encouraged by this regime and are valuable as food sources for some fritillary butterflies. The trimmed shrubs at the woodland edge are deliberately a mixture of deciduous and conifers and favour butterflies like speckled wood and white admiral which like this type of habitat.

In early summer look out for small, crimson, pea-like flowers amongst the grass. This is grass vetchling which has grass-like 'leaves' although these are modified stems. At other times of the year it is hard to find amongst the grass.

Several species of conifers have been planted including Norway spruce, cypress and western hemlock. The thick screen is good daytime shelter for large populations of muntjac and fallow deer, which you may sometimes see crossing paths or in quiet isolated areas. The conifers also provide a home for the tiny gold-crest, a smaller relation of the wren which feeds on insects in the trees. In recent years, crossbills have been seen here; as their name suggests, the two halves of this bird's beak cross over to act as a perfect tool for opening cones and extracting the seeds. Not all the trees are conifers though, and in autumn the changing colours of the broad-leaved deciduous trees add variety to the woodland.

2 SP609112

The ride eventually reaches a T-junction with a field visible straight ahead. Turn left here and after about one hundred metres climb the stile to the right into a meadow. Please keep to the path along the left side. This is Bernwood Meadow, a BBONT reserve and Site of Special Scientific Interest.

The field must have been arable land long ago as the ridge-and- furrow testifies but now the diversity of the plants found in the meadow indicates that this is very old grassland. In late spring there are large numbers of green-winged orchids in flower, while yellow rattle can be seen throughout the summer. This latter plant is semi-parasitic; its roots attach to grass roots and absorb nutrients which can considerably reduce the growth of the grass. After flowering, the ripe seeds roll about in the seed capsule until shaken out by the wind, the noise giving the plant its name. Some plants have prefer-

Orange tip on cuckoo flower

ences for different types of ground conditions. Notice how cuckoo flower, with delicate mauve flowers, likes the moisture in the furrows while the slender meadow buttercup prefers slightly drier conditions. The hay is harvested in July followed by grazing, the traditional way of using flower-rich meadows.

3 SP608107

At the end of the field climb over the stile on the left and continue in roughly the same direction through a scrubby area, then along the edge of a narrow field keeping the hedge on your right.

This grassland is not managed on a regular basis as the rough tussocks of grass, docks, thistles and meadow sweet demonstrate, a marked contrast to the well-managed meadow seen earlier.

Walk in the same direction through the woodland and continue until the road is reached.

This area of woodland is called Hell Coppice and the field on the right, Hell's Kitchen. It is thought that this was the site for brick kilns in the sixteenth century and these names may have originated at this time. The deciduous trees on the right may be remnants of the original woodland and the spring flowers like primrose, wood spurge, ransoms and bluebells would support this. In contrast, the conifers, with their close planting and dense foliage, produce a deep shade which eliminates most plants from beneath them. However, large numbers of small, pale, toadstools grow on the fallen needles. Many fungi have a close association with conifer roots for their mutual benefit, the fungi passing on minerals from the soil to the trees which in turn provide sugars for the fungi.

At the road turn right.

SHORT CUT Turn left and walk along the road to rejoin the trail at point 5.

Green-winged orchid

Soldier beetles on wild parsnip

At the junction the trail turns left down a grassy track, part of the Oxfordshire Way.

One noticeable plant growing along this pathway is wild parsnip. It is related to cow parsley and hogweed and is one of the few yellow flowered, umbelliferous plants (so named because of the flat-topped flower head, or umbel, of this group). As the name implies this plant is related to the cultivated parsnip and the root looks and smells like the vegetable. In the hedges are occasional bushes of wild privet. The strong-smelling clusters of white flowers are well liked by bees and flies and in winter the black berries are eaten by starlings and blackbirds which have to be acrobatic to reach the fruit at the end of the long flexible stems.

At the end of the lane go through the gate and turn right following the line of the woodland edge of Waterperry Wood.

Although this wood, and those walked through earlier, are now called Bernwood Forest, this name is taken from the old Royal Forest of Bernwood which originally covered a large area of Buckinghamshire north of here. It was at its largest extent during the reign of Richard I (1189-99) and its history is thought to stretch back to the Iron Age as part of a huge, multiple estate centred on Brill. It is likely that these two present day woodland areas were within the bounds of the Royal Forest until the late thirteenth century. In the Middle Ages the forest was important as a source of venison for the King and deer to stock parks elsewhere. It was also an important source of timber with large beams, arched crucks and joists being made from the oak here. There is also evidence of underwood provided from coppicing, as well as grazing rights for local villagers including some from Otmoor. Over the centuries the woodland was gradually reduced in extent, the land being cleared for more agriculture. In 1622 James I formally initiated the disafforestation of Bernwood Forest and the remaining woodland went into private ownership (see Introduction).

These open fields next to thick woodland are often used by grazing deer. Look out for muddy gaps along the woodland edge, the two-toed tracks marking deer paths; you may hear the roar of rutting fallow deer in autumn.

The variation in autumn tree colours can be seen well here, with reddish oaks in the woodland and yellow poplar and willow across the field. The green colour of the leaves is lost in autumn as the trees absorb the chlorophyll to re-use the following spring. This reveals underlying red and yellow pigments which protect the leaves from damaging sunlight radiation. When their important constituents have been stored, the leaves are dropped from the trees so that the trees can conserve moisture which may be in short supply in freezing weather. In contrast, the hard waxy needles of conifers lose much less water so are not shed in winter but are renewed constantly over several years.

The path bends to the left round the bottom of the wood; this area was earlier called Polecat's Corner although whether these animals were ever found here is unknown.

These fields are likely to contain grazing cattle. Notice the changes in agricultural practice which reflect changes in consumer demand. Until relatively recently, most cattle herds in this area were black-and-white Friesians, a good breed for milk and beef. With a demand for leaner meat, continental breeds such as Limousin and Charolais have been introduced and now many multi-coloured herds of these 'muscular animals' are to be seen. If you see Friesians, notice how each one has a unique pattern of black and white patches on its coat. This unique individual marking mirrors fingerprint patterns in humans.

4 SP609086

At the end of the field, take the track through the gate onto the lane.

This is a wide path with lots of tall grasses, flowering plants and shrubs such as dog rose and brambles. To the left on the forest edge are small trees including blackthorn, host plant to hairstreak butterflies with a tell-tale white line on the underwing. To the right on the field edge are willows. In early spring look closely at them and notice that the yellow male catkins (pussy willow) occur on different trees to the green, spiky female flowers. Both are useful food for early emerging bumblebees and other insects. In summer look for the similarity between the flowers of dog rose, bramble and yellow-flowered silverweed along the path. They all have five petals and many pollen bearing stamens and are all members of the rose family.

Further along, the track becomes a surfaced lane. Where the hedge is trimmed on the left look out for the small trees left uncut. These are wild service trees and more can be seen later. This area, now farmland, was once common grazing land belonging to the parish of Waterperry and the now-vanished hamlets of Thomley and Ledall. It was a valuable resource for the poor of the village as in the fifteenth and sixteenth centuries most of the arable land had been enclosed for sheep pasture, so limiting the land available for rough grazing.

Wild service tree

In the eighteenth century the Curson family, who were landowners, tried to enclose the common without making allotment or payment in lieu to the commoners and the Vicar. There was a bitter controversy with the Vicar, who was upset at his loss of money. Waterperry Common was finally enclosed later that century. In 1812 there was a small school here for the children who lived in the cottages nearby as the roads were too bad for them to get to the school in Waterperry. The name of Commonleys Farm reminds us of the past history of this small area.

5 SP618098

Short cut rejoins here

Turn right at the road and walk along until you reach a stile on the left about level with Dutch barns on the right. Take the path diagonally left across the field. Cross the plank bridge and stile, turn right and follow the field edge to the next stile on the right. Cross this and the bridge and walk straight on up the length of two fields. Climb another stile into a large field which gradually narrows leading to a stile and on into Shabbington Wood.

This woodland was used productively for many years after the end of the Royal Forest. Coppicing over a cycle of years produced a steady supply of

Trametes bracket fungus

small wood for faggots used in ovens and kilns, and bark from the felled oak was sold for tanning. As late as the Second World War charcoal was made for furnaces of the armaments industry in the Midlands. During both wars most usable timber was felled, leaving the woodland, in forestry terms, in a run down state, although it was recognised as an important site for wildlife by naturalists. In the 1950's the Shabbington and Waterperry Woods were taken over by the Forestry Commission who cleared most of the old woodland and scrub. Some of this clearance involved the use of strong chemical sprays before the areas were replanted with the mixture of trees seen now.

Continue straight on up a grassy path, cross a wide track and follow a forestry gravel track in the same direction as before. After a short time the track becomes grassy again and after a slight bend you will reach a crossroads of rides. Turn left here beside a wooden tower and continue until you can see a field through the trees on the right.

Look out for the whorls of brownish *Trametes*

bracket fungus which rots away the tree stumps by secreting powerful digestive enzymes.

When you reach the next observation tower turn left and then at the next junction turn right onto a gravel track.

At a large open intersection of tracks, opposite an information board and bench, notice the tall trees on your left. These are wild service trees which are good indicators of ancient woodland. They are generally rare in Oxfordshire but several remain in this wooodland complex, having escaped destruction when the plantations were formed.

Continue straight on in the same direction as before along the track which will lead back to the carpark.

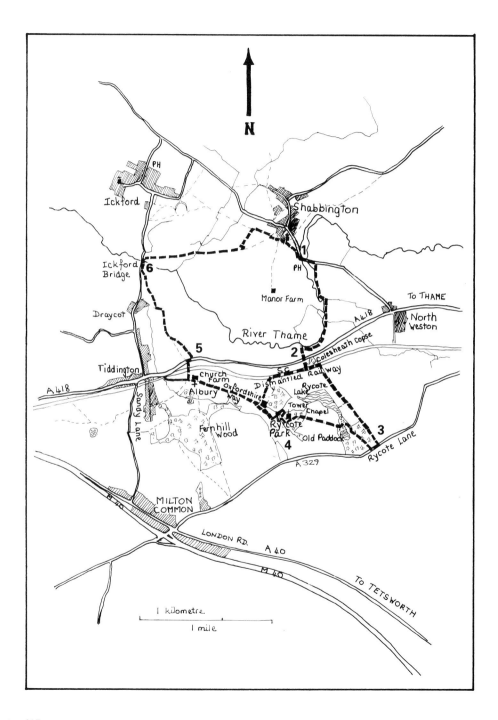

WALK 9
Rycote
5.5 miles 9 km
Short cut 4.5 miles 7 km

This walk follows an attractive stretch of the River Thame before passing through Rycote Park with its historic chapel. Continuing along part of the Oxfordshire Way the trail leads to the tiny hamlet of Albury and on through fields back to the river at Ickford Bridge. The path leads across pasture fields back to Shabbington. Easy walking throughout.

1 SP668065

Start from the Old Fisherman public house on the banks of the River Thame on the outskirts of Shabbington. Cross the bridge and pause for a moment to look at the river.

The clear water runs over a stony bottom here and you may see trout. Notice how they position themselves with their heads facing upstream. Trout need a high oxygen level and this is why they are only found in running water. If the weather is hot they move to deeper pools or to faster flowing water where the oxygen levels remain high; in other parts of the river the levels drop because of the temperature and increased use by aquatic plants. The presence of trout indicates that this water is relatively unpolluted and contains abundant insects for food.

Continue out of Shabbington and walk along the raised footway at the side of the road, over another branch of the river until a footpath is reached on the right leading off along the edge of a ditch. You will soon come to the River Thame which you follow for nearly a mile (1.5 km).

The raised path along the road indicates that this immediate area between two branches of the river is prone to flooding. These first fields are likely to be sheep grazed and have been used for pasture since the early sixteenth century, possibly because frequent flooding would have ruined arable crops.

Walking alongside the river there is plenty to see. Growing up from the river bed are large patches of dark green stems turning brown in autumn. These are bulrush, a true rush not to be confused with reedmace (often called bulrush) which will be seen later along the walk.

In spring listen for sedge warblers, small pale brown birds with a long, cheerful flowing song. They make their nests above the water, woven between the rush stems. Another commonly occurring bird here is the reed bunting. The males have bright reddy-brown backs and distinctive black heads. They may be quite conspicuous perched at the top of a reed stem or bush singing with a rather grating voice compared to that of the sedge warblers. The buntings nest in the bushes at the river side. Larger waterbirds like swan and mallard also nest here and in winter this part of the river is a rich site for visiting water fowl, including occasional rarities. Don't approach the swans too closely as they can be aggressive. The broken freshwater mussel shells which can be spotted along the field edge have been taken from the water by herons.

The river bank is also rich in insect life. As well as the mayflies seen briefly for a few days in May (see Walk 3) you may find a very spectacular damsel fly called the banded agrion or banded demoiselle. The male is a bright metallic blue with a dark patch on the centre of his wings while the female is metallic

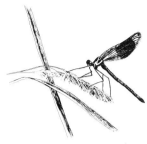

green with pale green wings without a dark patch. This is a predominantly southern species occurring in fast flowing streams with muddy bottoms. The males often perch on top of the streamside plants and are very active, often chasing each other over the water. You may see a male courting a female by fluttering his wings as he hovers in front of her. Other damsel flies to look out for are the blue-tailed, mostly black with a blue patch at the end of its body and one of the commonest British species. Look also for the azure, which as its name suggests is sky blue.

Banded demoiselle damselfly

2   SP668055

Eventually the path makes a sharp left-hand bend away from the river, following the line of a ditch and leading to the road close by.

This is a good place to see reedmace whose flat blue-green leaves are quite different from the bulrush in the river. The sausage shaped flowerheads are often pulled apart for nesting material by birds.

The young trees planted alongside the ditch are alder. The small cone structures are female flowers, the black ones are from last year and the green ones

Reedmace

Alder

are this year's. The male flowers are long red catkins formed in autumn, which drop off after the pollen has been released in late winter. Alder is a characteristic tree of river banks and wet places, its water tolerant wood was used in the past for making objects which were subject to repeated wetting such as broomheads and clogs.

Meadow brown on ox-eye daisy

Cross the busy A418 with care and take the path facing you. Continue straight on following the field edge. Very soon it climbs up a steep embankment where you turn left.

Short cut returns to this point

This bank marks the line of a now disused railway. This was the extension of the Wycombe line to Oxford opened as broad gauge in 1864, converted to narrow gauge in 1870. The line was closed to passenger traffic in 1963 and the track lifted in 1969, having had a useful life of about a hundred years. This makes an interesting contrast with the history of the two roads which will be crossed during this walk. The A418 was only a bridleway until at least 1823 but now is the main route between Aylesbury and Oxford. Another busy road to be met later, which lies over the fields to the right, is Rycote Lane. As long ago as 1345 it was deemed to be important enough for part to be rebuilt as a stone causeway, paid for by a Thame merchant, possibly to facilitate transport of goods to the market at Thame. In 1768 this route was made into a turnpike between Aylesbury and Little Milton and now, as the A329, links Thame with the M40.

Perennial rye grass

Soft brome

The plants to be found on the old railway embankment are typical of dry poor soil in contrast to the lush growth alongside the river and ditches. Look out for creeping cinquefoil with five leaflets, yellow flowered members of the daisy family like cat's ears and hawkbits, white ox-eye daisy and a vetch, the small, mauve flowered tare. To the left is a patch of woodland known as Colesheath Copse.

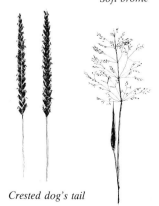

Crested dog's tail

Velvet bent

Sweet vernal grass

Cock's foot

Timothy

Yorkshire fog

Barren brome

Several English oaks border the path. See how the leaves have very short stalks with two small backward projections at the base. The acorns are carried on long stalks from which derives the alternative name of pedunculate oak. In the north of England the common oak is the sessile oak with long stalked leaves, without the baseal projections and unstalked, or sessile, acorns. Sometimes the two types hybridise to produce an intermediate form.

At the end of the woodland take the path to the right along the field edge and continue across three fields to the road.

In early summer notice how many different types of grasses occur in what at first sight seems to be a uniform grass field. Their flower heads help to differentiate them. Unlike many flowering plants, grasses grow from the base of the plant, so that any damage to the tops by grazing or cutting still allows regrowth. This is why grass is used for lawns. These grasses are relatives of valuable cereal crops like wheat, barley, oats and rice. New techniques of plant breeding and genetic engineering allow useful characteristics, such as disease resistance, to be transferred from wild species to cultivated, agricultural ones.

In winter when the grass is short you can see a good example here, of ridge and furrow. The boundary between two furlongs can clearly be seen where the ridges change direction (see Introduction).

3   SP677044

Continue to the road and turn right for a short distance. Be wary of the fast traffic. Take a path to the right marked Oxfordshire Way into woodland.

This woodland is called Old Paddock but from the evidence of old maps it seems likely that only a small portion has been unwooded during the last two hundred years at least. This first part of the wood is light and the poplar trees well spaced, thus allowing plenty of light to the ground flora below. The ground is quite damp which favours several sedges found here such as lesser pond and fox sedge. Many trees are encrusted with lichen, some forming flat growths and others which have an erect branching form. Lichens are made up of two components, algae and fungi, which grow together in a specially adapted form to benefit them both.

Further on through the wood the tree cover changes from willow and poplar to hornbeam. Some have several trunks showing that they were coppiced at some time in the past. They produce a far denser shade; notice how the ground cover is now reduced to shade tolerant plants such as wood avens (Herb Bennet) and Herb Robert. Many of the fallen trees have a variety of fungi growing on them, especially

Rycote chapel

Lichen covered tree bark

noticeable in autumn and winter, which help speed up the decay of the dead wood.

Follow the path out of the woodland across an arable field to more woodland. When the house is in view, bear left through the trees towards Rycote Chapel and a very large old yew.

Rycote is mentioned in the Domesday Book and the village of Rycote Magna had at least 22 families in 1279. However between 1450 and 1700 the hamlet disappeared, leaving only the house and chapel. Rycote Chapel was built in the mid 15th century by the Quatremain family who owned the estate and is well worth a visit (telephone 0272 734472 for opening times). The house which stood nearby was rebuilt in a grand style in the sixteenth century and the grounds were landscaped by Capability Brown in 1769 for the Earl of Abingdon. The Great House was burnt to the ground soon afterwards leaving only the stable block which was restored early this century and converted to the house seen here today.

4 SP664046

Past the chapel follow the track to the left and take a path off to the right over a stile and cross a small field bearing right to emerge on to a farm road. Go through the yard and continue in the same general direction.

SHORT CUT Turn right at the end of the farm yard taking the road down hill to return to the disused railway line. Turn right along the bank until the path on the left from the road is reached (point 2). Retrace your steps to Shabbington along the river bank.

Follow the track as it leads down and then up to Albury. There are wide views to the right over the river valley towards Brill on the hilltop.

The tiny hamlet of Albury has always been small but has existed since early Saxon days. The name means 'old fortified place' which implies an even earlier settlement. The fields around the hamlet were enclosed well before 1685 and by 1813 the grassland was notable for dairy production.

This old track from Rycote to Albury leads close to the church which was rebuilt in 1830, at the Earl of Abingdon's expense, to replace the old one demolished two years earlier.

Opposite the buildings of Church Farm, now used as offices, look for the path over a stile between two wooden sheds on the left. Turn right and walk down the road taking the signed path on the right opposite Albury Grange and beside a house. Walk downhill through a field and cross the old railway cutting, continuing to the road.

Some interesting plants can be seen along this stretch of the walk, probably garden escapes. Look out for Scots thistle at the end of the garden on the right, a large plant with pale green stems and very spiky leaves. In the railway cutting several plants of caper spurge can be seen, so named because of the resemblance of the seed capsules to capers, although they are not related and are not edible.

5 SP651051

At the road turn right and, taking care, walk to a lay-by on a bend in the road. Here look for the path off to the left which leads into a field. Follow this, keeping the hedge on your right until a gate is reached. At the gate bear right and walk down a broad grassy track between two hedges.

This track leads to Draycot, now no more than a small group of farm buildings and a couple of houses. Like Rycote and Albury this is an example of what is termed by historians a 'shrunken village'. Gradually, between 1450 and 1700, these hamlets reduced in size but never actually disappeared, as happened in many other places. These few houses and the green track are remnants of the once larger settlement.

Before the farmyard gate, turn right and follow

the concrete farm road, branching off to the right along the field edge towards the poplar plantation.

The silvery-grey leaves of some of these trees are characteristic of white poplar. Poplars are members of the willow family and tend to prefer damp places where they grow rapidly. The timber is very light and resistant to splintering, hence its use in the past for wagon bases and packing cases.

Continue along this edge, through another field to the river where a narrow path leads off to the left, over a stile and footbridge and up steps to the road.

6 SP649064

Turn right along the road and on to the bridge. Look out for the stone dated 1685 set into the wall that marks the county boundary between Oxfordshire and Buckinghamshire. The bridge site is much older than this though and dates from at least 1237 when it was mentioned in records as a wooden structure repaired with oak from Brill Wood. From the bridge a good view can be had of the river and surrounding fields.

Along the river are pollarded willows, their tops regularly cut off in the past to provide flexible poles for fencing and other farm uses. The roots spread along the riverbank and form an interlocking web which helps to prevent the soil in the riverside fields from washing away. Beyond the river is a round pool fed by drainage ditches. In early summer you will see yellow water-lily growing here. The bridge which crosses this pond is called Whirlpool Arch so perhaps in times of flood this pool was less peaceful than now. The earthworks in the field beyond the pool are thought to be a cavalry trench dug by Cromwell's forces during the Civil War.

Over the bridge climb the stile on the right and follow the path diagonally left across the field and through a gap in the hedge. Continue in roughly the same direction to a stile. Look out for the way marks. After a time the path crosses a wooden bridge and leads along a field edge to a stony track. Turn left here and then right just before a brick building. Walk diagonally left to the far corner of this field and then bear right heading for a track beside a bungalow.

Go into the field opposite where you can make a detour on the left to see Shabbington Church of St Mary Magdalene which has several interesting medieval features. It was built in about 1160 on the site of an earlier building and is a rare example of architecture derived from earlier Saxon designs. The field itself is full of bumps and hollows where, it is reputed, the old manor house stood.

Continue across the field to return to the starting point.

Acknowledgements

This book was written and researched by Mary Webb, Alan Spicer and Allister Smith, all of the Oxford Polytechnic and was illustrated by Louise Spicer.

The authors are grateful for help and support from the Oxfordshire County Museum Services and Berkshire, Buckinghamshire and Oxfordshire Naturalists Trust (BBONT), for advice on geology from Alan Childs and for photographic assistance by Barbara Southall.

The project was sponsored by Oxfordshire County Council.